TUSCANY

past and present

BARNES
&NOBLE
BOOKS
NEW YORK

TUSCANY

past and present

Texts
Costanza Poli

Design
Alberto Bertolazzi

Editing Supervision by
Valeria Manferto De Fabianis

Translation by
Neil Frazer Davenport

Art Director
Patrizia Balocco Lovisetti

1 The Calcio Storico is one of the oldest and most popular of the traditional Florentine festivals. The participants dress in Renaissance costumes and represent the four city quarters, San Giovanni, Santa Croce, Santa Maria Novella and Santo Spirito. Prior to the matches, drummers and flag twirlers stir up the crowd.

2-7 The volutes that enhance the facade of Santa Maria Novella in Florence were designed by Leon Battista Alberti: geomtrical patterns and floral decorations combine ine the soft classical motif that characterises the marble of one of the most beautiful Tuscan churches.

3-6 The golden yellow of the Sienese earth spreads over rolling hills punctuated by farmhouses. Like silent sentinels, the cypresses, unmistakable symbols of the Tuscan countryside, rise to mark a border or shade a winding road.

© 1996 White Star S.r.l.
Via C. Sassone, 22/24 -
13100 Vercelli, Italy.

This edition published by
Barnes & Noble, Inc.,
by arrangement with
White Star S.r.l.,
2001 Barnes & Noble Books

ISBN 0-7607-2397-4
M1098765432

Colour separations by
Gai Scaligera, Verona.
Printed in Italy by
Grafedit, Bergamo.

CONTENTS

*T*uscany resists definition: in the global collective consciousness it is the Italian region par excellence and, even in its multifaceted diversity, it represents a cohesive historical, artistic and naturalistic entity that just happens to be situated right in the center of the peninsula. What follows are brief notes on the history and culture of the region. Rather than being comprehensive accounts, they are intended to act as spurs and invitations, to compel you to follow those twisting roads that wind their way among rolling hills, to lose yourselves in the labyrinthine streets and alleys of the medieval cities, to dream in front of a Tyrrhenian sunset as you stroll along the endless beaches of the Maremma or to contemplate the sea from the rocky shore of Elba. You are also invited to listen to the vernacular of the native Tuscans and to examine their faces for traces of their Etruscan or Roman forebears, to participate in the festivals and games that have long marked the return of spring, the veneration of saints and ancient battles and heroic enterprises. Visiting Tuscany is something of an obligatory rite of passage, and the region has something to offer to us all. Art here is no isolated monument, no single noble palace or solitary stela. It is something that

8 top Monteriggioni, the ancient Sienese outpost that was intended to halt the Florentine advance, is now a tranquil country town rising suddenly from the crown of a hill. The old town walls — reinforced by 14 square towers that were once much taller—conceal a fragment of medieval Tuscany that has remained virtually unchanged.

permeates and is an indispensable, ineluctable aspect of everyday life. Here you can walk along roads worn by the feet of Giotto, Masaccio, Donatello and Michelangelo. Gaze at the banks of the Arno and you evoke memories of Dante, Boccaccio and Petrarch. The villas immersed in the countryside were the settings for the intellectual indulgences of Cosimo and Lorenzo dei Medici and the twilight years of Machiavelli. It was in the duomo at Pisa that Galileo Galilei had the intuition that changed the course of scientific thought. The Tuscan countryside has a perhaps less academic culture to relate, but one no less rich and varied. Over thousands of years agriculture has created a landscape so instantly recognizable that the term "Tuscan hills" has come to describe the exemplary molding of nature by the hand of humans. You can hardly visit the great cities of art and ignore the Sienese *Crete,* the *calanchi* of Pratomagno and the tufa hills of Grosseto. The Tuscan civilization has, moreover, always had a gently influential role, capable of showing the way, of developing an idea to its peak before withdrawing and leaving to others the task of exhausting its potential while it concentrates on inventing something new. It was thus in the fields of art and lit-

8-9 Montalcino, an ancient town perched atop a hill covered with vineyards and olive groves, looks out over the lush green Val d'Orcia. Today the name of this small town appears on the most sophisticated tables around the world thanks to Brunello di Montalcino, a fine wine that gives nothing away to its rivals from Bordeaux.

9 top The center of Lucignano, close to Monte San Savino, has retained the elliptical form dictated by the morphology of the hill on which it sits. The enchanting landscape of the Valdichiana extends in all directions.

10-11 "The conceptual meaning of Botticelli's Primavera *will be clear only to philosophers or initiates. However, we can all see it in the agreeableness of the woods and flower-strewn lawn, in the seductive beauty of the bodies and faces, in the fluidity of the lines, in the delicate harmony of the colors." Giulio Carlo Argan,* Storia dell'Arte Italiana.

14-15 The Ponte Vecchio in Florence is much more than a means of crossing from one side of the Arno to the other: it is a symbol of the city's enduring strength, an important commercial center and a favorite stroll for elegant ladies and youngsters with knapsacks and guitars.

16-17 The Campo dei Miracoli in Pisa is not merely a piazza containing some of the finest examples of Romanesque architecture: the green of the grass lawns and the white of the marble contribute to a unique and perfect whole in which the extraordinary "imperfection" of the leaning tower appears quite at home.

18-19 The Duomo of Siena, dressed in black and white marble, emerges from the medieval heart of the city. The present cathedral was, in the grandiose plans of the city council, intended to be just the transept of an immense church.

erature in bygone centuries. Revolutions are not always the prerogatives of men of arms, at times all it takes is a man of creative genius to change the course of cultural history. In championing the Tuscan vernacular over Latin and the other idioms, Dante changed the history of the Italian language; turning his back on Byzantine iconography, Giotto introduced human passion to the representation of the divine. And, almost 500 years after the event, the scientific discoveries of Leonardo are still being studied. Today a similar process can be observed in terms of our perception of the quality of Tuscan life. Never before has a country house in Tuscany been so highly sought. The metropolises are being rejected as people seek out the peace and fresh greenery of the countryside or try to enter into the daily life of small towns that contain more works of art than the average European city. These immigrants are the last of a legion: ever since Roman times the dream of the serenity of Tuscan provincial life has captivated millions. The true Tuscans look on these would-be producers of olive oil and wine, barn restorers and holiday farm entrepreneurs with a hint of ironic sufferance. "Tuscanity" is not something that can be learned; it is a quality imbibed directly from mother's milk along with the aspirated Tuscan "c," a typical pronunciation of the region.

Uccellina National Park

Alpi
Apuane

Carrara
Massa

Ligurian Sea

Viareggio

Appennino Tosco-Emiliano

Pistoia

Prato

Montecatini
Terme

Florence

Serchio

Lago di
Massaciuccoli

Lucca

Pisa

Arno

Empoli

Scandicci

San
Miniato

Livorno

San Gimignano

Arezzo

Isola di
Gorgona

Volterra

Cortona

Cecina

Siena

Cecina

Montepulciano

Montalcino

Civitella

Chianciano
Terme

Isola di
Capraia

Piombino

Follonica

Portoferraio

Gulf of
Follonica

Bruna

Ombrone

Isola
d'Elba

Porto
Azzurro

Grosseto

Tuscan
Archipelago

Monti
dell'Uccellina

Albegna

Lago di
Orbetello

Isola di
Pianosa

Porto
Santo
Stefano

Orbetello

Isola di
Montecristo

Isola
del Giglio

Monte
Argentario

Port'Ercole

Tyrrhenian Sea

Isola di
Giannutri

The Vernaccia vinyards with San Gimignano in the background.

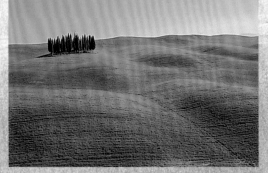

The Sienese hills.

The Ponte Vecchio, Florence.

The Duomo of Siena

Piazza dei Miracoli at Pisa.

HISTORY

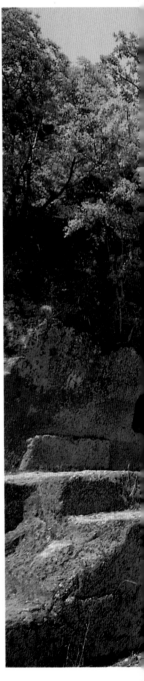

To the Romans they were known as the *Tusci* or the *Etruschi* while to the Greeks they were the *Tyrrhenians*: what is clear is that the Etruscans are the ancestors of the modern Tuscans, even though only a few of the most important centers of their ancient civilization lay within the current boundaries of the region. The original Etruria comprised the area between the Arno and the Tevere rivers and thus included broad sweeps of both Umbria and Lazio, while excluding the modern-day Tuscan provinces of Massa Carrara and Lucca, which were then Ligurian territory. One theory regarding the origin of the Etruscan people goes back to Herodotus and the state of Lydia from where they fled shortly after the Trojan War. Another has the Etruscans descending from Tyrrhenian-Pelasgian pirates, while Latin historian Livy claimed that they had arrived from regions beyond the Alps. More recent theses claim that the Etruscans were the result of a fusion between the native people and immigrants from the East. What is of most interest is the cultural supremacy achieved by the Etruscans. They created a sophisticated civilization that reached its peak in the 7th century BC, when the power and wealth of the Etruscan aristocracy allowed the importation of products in gold, silver, ivory and bronze from the East, from Egypt and from Greece. The gradual decline of this civilization—partly caused by military defeats—and the final coup de grâce provided by the rise of Rome destroyed a society that today we know of only through indirect sources, archaeological finds and historical accounts. The Etruscan cities, such as Vetulonia, Populonia, Volterra and Arezzo to name but four, were city-states comparable to the Greek polis and dominated the surrounding lands with alliances, a fragmentation that made a major contribution to their eventual demise. The triumph of Rome and the reduction of Etruria to the status of a province were confirmed with the construction of two consular roads. The Via Aurelia ran along the coast while the interior was served by the Via Cassia that linked Bolsena, Chiusi and Arezzo. The Apennines and the Arno River were the natural barriers to the two arteries that terminated at Luni and Fiesole. A third road, the Clodia, entered into the heart of Etruria and joined up with the Via Aurelia. These routes are still valid and can be found unchanged as parts of the current Tuscan road network. Well off these tracks the Romans established military bases that became great cities of art and arms: Lucca, Pistoia, Florence and Pisa all conserve the structure of the Roman *castrum*, with its *cardo* and *decumano*.

20-21 The tomb of Ildebrand in the Etruscan necropolis at Sovana, one of the tufa towns in the province of Grosseto. This is one of the best preserved tombs in an area in which there are numerous traces of the settlements of the ancient civilization.

21 top The grandiose Roman theater at Volterra dates back to imperial times. Parts of the stage, the cavea and the portico remain, the latter containing a thermal bath. Among the wealth of Etruscan remains in the area is Velathri, the city of alabaster.

21 top right The Arco Gate at Volterra is inserted into the remains of massive walls and faces out over the valley.

21 bottom right The Tomb of the Pilgrim in the Etruscan necropolis carved into the tufa at Chiusi contains sarcophagi and funerary urns. It is one of the most famous burial sites, along with the Scimmia and Colle tombs. The search for the legendary Porsenna tomb described by the ancient writers has proven fruitless.

Following the fall of the Roman Empire in the West, the invasions by Theodoric and the wars between the Ostrogoths and the Byzantines weakened the Tuscia region and in the middle of the 6th century the Longobards were able to walk in unopposed. It was however, this conquest that marked the beginning of the rebirth of the region. The protracted Longobard dominion (until 774) saw, above all, a growth in the importance of Lucca. Chosen as a ducal fiefdom, the city was linked to the Padana plain via the Cisa Pass. At the same the influence of Pisa also expanded and the city became a major trading power from its Tyrrhenian base. The accession to power of Charlemagne marked the onset of an administrative "revolution" and confirmed the influence of the bishops who wielded both spiritual and secular power. Under the Carolingians the number of castles devoted to the defense of the region increased, and after the year 1000 the region witnessed a period of growth. The first effect of this turn of events was the building of new churches. With the help of the faithful, it was the local aristocrats who promoted this religious building spree: there began a noble race to erect the largest abbey, the most popular convent, the most venerated chapel. Then there were the *pievi*, a kind of country parish directly dependent on the bishoprics; the *pievi* enjoyed great privileges in the 11th century. Here the faithful were baptised and buried and also saw justice administered. Even though they were situated outside the inhabited centers, the *pievi* immediately became poles of attraction. While many of the ancient coastal towns such as Luni, were abandoned, Pisa went from strength to strength as via its port it maintained contacts with Corsica, Sardinia and the coast of North Africa, laying the basis for the Marine Republic. Feudal Tuscany was a conglomerate of potentates, frequently led by bishops with all the power of earls, making it more of a mosaic than a united region. It was this structure that allowed the communes to develop, and then demand political and cultural autonomy. In the meantime another element, religion, began to change the face of the region. The foundation of the Orders of the Camoldolesi and the Vallombrosani were to have great influence over Tuscan life and its history. At the center of these events were the great cities that began their struggle for preeminence, prior to demolishing the remaining traces of the Tuscan marquisate. Feudalism continued to exist only in the poorest areas such as the Lunigiana, the Casentino, the Val Tiberina and part of the Maremma; the future of Tuscany lay with the city-states.

22 The Basilica di San Francesco at Assisi was undoubtedly built to the greater glory of the saint, but it is also true that the work of Giotto is so extensive and successful here that the building might well have been dedicated at least in part to the artist. This illustration shows a scene from the episode in which St. Francis drives the demons from Arezzo. Given the realism employed by the artist, it is reasonable to suppose that this is a reliable record of the city in the 14th century.

23 top A work by Domenico Lenzi, known as il Biadaiolo, conserved in the Laurenziana Library in Florence, reveals the wealthy and industrious appearance of the 14th-century city in which every inhabitant, men women and priests, had clearly defined roles.

23 bottom In the sacristy of San Miniato al Monte in Florence there is a fresco cycle by Spinello Aretino and his pupils dedicated, above all, to the figure of San Benedetto. In this scene the saint recognizes King Totila.

24 top left *The battle of Montaperti— illustrated by Giovanni di Ventura in a codex in the City Library at Siena— took place on the 4th September 1260, and was fought between the Guelphs of Florence and the Ghibellines of Siena. The battle, recorded by Dante in the 10th and 32nd cantos of his* Inferno, *was won by the Ghibellines, who consigned the Guelphs to exile.*

24 top right *The gold florin, minted for the first time in Florence in 1252, was the symbol of the economic primacy of Florence throughout Tuscany and of its international prestige.*

The Tuscan cities were free of, or at least attempted to maintain their autonomy from, the authority of the papacy and the empire, although they did align themselves with one or the other. This situation represented the birth of the communes, and Florence, Pisa, Siena, Lucca and Arezzo competed among themselves, gradually eliminating the feudal territories. The "Queen" of the 13th century was Pisa. The city participated in the Crusades, mounted a raid against the Moors in the Balearics and attempted to expand, although defeat at Meloria (1284) against the Genoans marked the beginning of its decline. At the same time began the irresistible rise of Florence that even in the early years of the century had begun to undermine the economic power of Siena, which until that moment had been the "bank" of the Holy See. The conflict between the Guelphs and the Ghibellines, the most significant event in Tuscany in the 13th century, is proof that the struggle for power in the region was between two well-defined social strata. The great noble families, stripped of their feudal rights, were unwilling to accept the rise of their rivals, the mercantile class, the bourgeoisie, who were unwilling to accept the interference of the empire in their affairs and development. The Guelphs were to prevail, following the Ghibellines' brief victory at Montaperti in 1260. Within this political climate the dominion of Florence also extended throughout much of the region. In the 14th century the city conquered, with arms or money, Arezzo, Prato and shortly afterwards Pisa, Cortona and Livorno. Wealthy in terms of gold and prestige—the gold *fiorino*, first minted in 1252, was already the dominant coin—Florence was searching for a leader who would put an end to the oligarchic government. She found this leader first in the charismatic figure of Cosimo dei Medici, also known as Cosimo the Elder, and then in Lorenzo il Magnifico.

24-25 Following his victory over Castruccio Castracani, the Sienese authorities commissioned Simone Martini, the painter of the Maestà *in the Palazzo Pubblico, to celebrate the virtues of Guidoriccio da Fogliano in a grandiose work of art. The hero of Monte Massi is portrayed alone between two conquered castles. Behind lies his camp, before him lies his triumph.*

25 The Guelph (bottom) and Gibelline (top) seals. The two factions fought for power in Italy between the 13th nd the 14th centuries, the former as supporters of the papacy, the latter in favor of the Holy Roman Empire. In reality, behind the formal positions lay intense personal rivalries between the two noble families.

26 top *The Codice Miniato of 1472, conserved in the State Archive at Siena, shows that trade, like all other activities, was controlled by precise norms. Good government was a blend of Liberalism and strict formal control.*

26 bottom *The Salone dei Cinquecento in the Palazzo Vecchio in Florence was built on the orders of Savonarola and was intended to house 500 councillors following the departure of the* Medici. *However, it was a Medici, Cosimo I, who commissioned Giorgio Vasari to extend the hall and decorate it with fresco panels celebrating the city. In this scene Pisa is being attacked by the Florentine troops.*

26-27 *The Sienese school of the 14th century boasted a long series of talented followers of Simone Martini and the Lorenzetti brothers: Bartolo di Fredi, in* this Adoration of the Magi, *now in the Pinacoteca Nazionale in Siena, shows a realistic glimpse of his city at the height of its glory.*

27 top This work by
Pontormo, now in the
Uffizi, shows an
idealized portrait of
Cosimo the Elder, an
extremely wealthy
businessman who
became the arbiter of
Florentine political
life, exercising a de
facto hegemony for 30
years and establishing
the Medici dynasty.

27 bottom This work,
in the Museo degli
Argenti in Florence,
represents the port of
Livorno in 1560. The
silting up of the port
of Pisa in the 16th
century favored the
development of
Livorno, which
became the most
important of the
Medici dominions.
Work on the port
continued up until
the beginning of the
17th century.

28 top
The martyrdom
of Girolamo
Savonarola.
His passionate
accusations of
corruption among the
clergy and politicians
and his fervent

demands for reform
and democracy led to
his excommunication
by Pope Alexander
VI in 1497. Arrested
and found guilty, he
was first hanged and
then his body was set
on fire.

28-29 Vincenzo
Rustici, the
Presentazione delle
Contrade in the
Piazza del Campo
and the Gioco con
Tori in Piazza del
Campo. The two
works show how deeply

sport is embedded in
the Sienese spirit. In
the shadow of the
Mangia Tower, in the
terracotta bowl of the
campo, every event
was—and still is—an
opportunity for
competition.

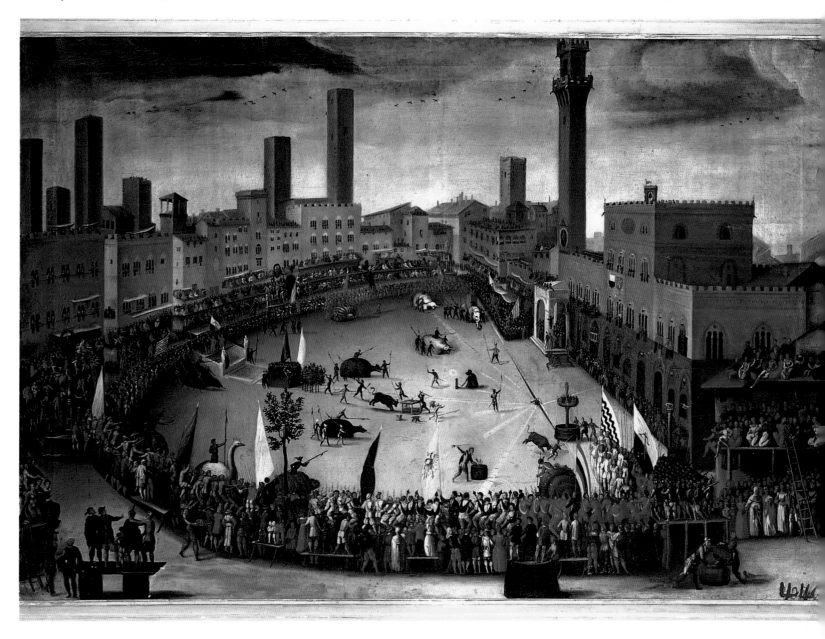

*L*orenzo il Magnifico was the latter, an astute and brilliant politician, the de facto lord of the city, who unified the Florentine dominions, providing them with a solid structure capable of resisting external influence. Subsequent events, with the government of Florence disputed between the promoters of the republican oligarchy and the Medici family, concluded with the rise to power of the first Grand Duke of Tuscany, Cosimo I, in 1537. The passage from the era of the communes to the authority of a recognized lord had been completed and for almost 40 years the activities of Cosimo I were inseparable from the development of Tuscany itself, as he governed the region with a sure and enthusiastic hand. His work contributed to the political unity of the area and the reforms set underway created an absolute state, but he was also responsible for streamlining the administrative structures and attempting to establish the equality of all Tuscan citizens before the law.

A personality as strong as that of Cosimo I inevitably overshadows those of his successors. Francesco Maria is of note above all for his interest in court life and his policy of strict observance of the pro-Spanish line. His brother Ferdinand, on the other hand was a cardinal who returned to secular life to occupy himself with the affairs of the state and preferred to seek the support of the French. He is best remembered for his work at Livorno and his attempts to reclaim certain marshy areas of the Grand Duchy. The Medici family's attempts to free them-selves of the Spanish hegemony continued under Cosimo II, while under Ferdinand II the region was struck by two great disasters, famine due to poor harvests and plague, as well as the unstoppable decline of its economic position. At this time only Livorno, with its grandiose, open port, escaped the effects of the general recession. The demise of the Medici dynasty was hastened by this climate of crisis and corruption, and on the death of Gian Gastone in 1737, the Grand Duchy eventually passed into the hands of the Bourbon of Spain and then into the hands of the House of Lorraine. This marked the end of the story of the Medici family, its period of great splendor followed by a long, tormented decline.

FIORENZA

30-31 Lorenzo il Magnifico portrayed among artists in a work by Ottavio Vannini. Lorenzo's fame as a patron of the arts was well deserved. Among his interests, in addition to literature, were the collection of antiquities and books, music and philosophy. Moreover, he promoted culture in the broadest sense by instituting the Studio Generale of Pisa.

31 top Florence at the end of the 15th century, reconstructed in a 19th-century painting conserved in the Topographical Museum. The city appears as a hive of activity and well-being surrounded by imposing walls.

32-33 The ideal of courtly love is well represented by Benozzo Gozzoli. In his work, Viaggio dei Magi, in the Palazzo Medici-Riccardi in Florence, he depicted Lorenzo dei Medici in the caravan of the three kings in all his usual magnificence, together with his family and trusted archers.

T he accession to the throne of Peter Leopold of Lorraine in 1765 marked the beginning of the rebirth of the territory. The young grand duke—he was just eighteen years old—looked to the grandiose figure of Cosimo for inspiration and was aided by illustrious collaborators, such as Pompeo Neri, Angelo Tavanti and Francesco Maria Gianni, supporters of a liberal economic policy. With the land reclamation in the Maremma, the Val de Chiana and around Pisa—via the excavation of canals, the reconstruction of the port of Castiglione della Pescaia and benefits conceded to those willing to settle in these areas—the improvements in the communications network with new routes through the Apennines being opened up, the administrative and judiciary reforms and the abolition of torture and the death penalty, over a period of 25 years Peter Leopold tried to drag Tuscany into the modern age. Among his initiatives was the renewal of the agricultural system with the auctioning of the Medici possessions, a reform that transformed Tuscany into a region of small landowners. Then there was the abolition of the art and craft corporations and an unsuccessful attempt to revive the manufacturing industry. This ambitious reforming program was crowned by a written constitution drawn up by Francesco Maria Gianni.

34 top Maria Luisa Bourbon, the wife of Charles IV of Spain, married Ludovico di Bourbon-Parma in 1795, and with him ascended to the throne of Etruria. Following the Napoleonic events and the Congress of Vienna, she was assigned the Duchy of Lucca, which she led with great energy.

34 bottom Francis I of the Holy Roman Empire; Francis Stephen, the Duke of Lorraine; Francis II, the Grand Duke of Tuscany and Duke of Parma and Piacenza, all legitimate titles for the son of the Duke of Lorraine. Leopold, in spite of being formally at the head of the Grand Duchy of Tuscany, never lived in Florence and was represented by a regency council.

34-35 Peter Leopold of Hapsburg-Lorraine, the Grand Duke of Tuscany from 1765 to 1790—portrayed here in a family group by Wilhelm Berczy—was a great reformer with a passion for civil and economic liberty, good and honest administration and local self-government. His masterpiece was a new penal code inspired by Beccaria that abolished torture and capital punishment.

35 top Charles VIII of France entered Florence in 1494 through the Porta San Frediano and was welcomed by the populace who had rebelled against the power of the Medici. In reality, Charles was only passing through Florence on his way to the Kingdom of Naples and, in 1512 the Florentine Medici family regained control of the city.

36 This watercolor by Terrani depicts a ball at Pisa held in honor of Peter Leopold I. Between 1778 and 1782 the grand duke promoted the development of a project for a political constitution based on electoral representation.
It was never put into practice as the grand duke was called to the Imperial throne at Vienna.

36-37 A palio in Siena dedicated to Francis II and Maria Theresa, the daughter of Charles IV. Having ascended to the throne following the extinction of the Medici line, and being but a mediocre ruler, Francis was to be remembered in Tuscany above all as the father of Peter Leopold.

38 top A painting by Emilio Burci dated 1868 shows the banks of the Arno, the Ponte alle Grazie and, to the top right, San Miniato al Monte. The Ponte alle Grazie was destroyed by the Germans during the Second World War after having resisted flooding for centuries. It was subsequently replaced by a modern construction.

38-39 Piazza Santa Croce, bordered by the basilica and the palazzi, has ever since the Middle Ages been the favorite site for celebrations, games and tournaments. This picture by Giovanni Signorini shows the Florentine carnival.

When Peter Leopold acceded to the imperial throne, he was succeeded by Ferdinand III. His long and troubled reign was marked by the Napoleonic period. During the French Revolution Tuscany maintained a neutral position in spite of the presence of a British fleet in the Tyrrhenian Sea and diplomatic pressure to join the anti-revolution coalition. In 1799 the Duchy of Lucca was invaded by the French troops: with the aristocratic republic declared void, a provisional government took power. The same happened in Florence following the departure of Ferdinand. This was a dark age for Tuscany, with popular uprisings in support of the restoration while in Siena there were even bonfires lit to burn the Jacobin followers. The Sanfedista "revolt" brought the grand duke back to the throne and shortly afterwards the Austrian troops put an end to the disorders. However, following the Treaty of Lunéville, the Grand Duchy was once again taken out of the hands of the House of Lorraine and the Bourbons of Parma were installed in Florence. Napoleon had changed the structure of the newborn Kingdom of Etruria with reforms and innovations brought in from France. The restoration had the effect of sweeping away the ephemeral dominion of Bonaparte and in 1815 the Congress of Vienna established the status of the Grand Duchy of Tuscany. Ferdinand III returned to the throne; his blood ties with the house of Austria determined his foreign policy, but in domestic terms he managed to create conditions of peace and tranquility with a degree of harmony. It was in this period that two of the most important institutions in Italian intellectual life were created, the Gabinetto Viessieux as well as the Accademia Georgofili, which dealt with the technical progress and development of the region. Leopold II, the grand duke from 1824, was a mild,

39 Piazza della Signoria in a 19th-century painting: the ladies in crinolines and the gentlemen in top hats have been replaced by the millions of tourists who swarm here to visit Florence, regarded as the shapely daughter of Rome.

tolerant sovereign who made Tuscany a secure asylum for exiled patriots, thus defusing attempts at internal rebellion. He was also responsible for the revival of the land reclamation schemes, the re-opening of the iron ore mine on Elba and, in 1847, for the annexation of the Duchy of Lucca. Freedom of the press and an official statute, as well as Tuscany's participation in the wars of independence, opened up the borders of the Grand Duchy, but the activities of extremist groups and the revolt at

Livorno led to Leopold's exile at Gaeta and shattered the good relations established between the grand duke—who abandoned Tuscany in 1859—and his subjects. The provisional government and the plebiscite of 1860 marked the region's absorption into the Kingdom of Sardinia. The new king entered Florence and between 1865 and 1870 the city was the capital of the Kingdom of Italy.

In conclusion, a few words on the

immense damage in terms of human life and works of art suffered by Tuscany and Florence in particular during the Second World War. On the night of August 3, 1944, all the bridges over the Arno with the exception of the Ponte Vecchio were destroyed. That one remaining link was, however, blocked by the rubble from the demolition of the surrounding medieval quarters, mined by the Germans during their retreat. Natural disasters led to the Arno bursting its banks in 1966, and in 1993 a terrorist bomb caused the deaths of innocent victims, destroyed the home of the Accademia dei Georgofili and badly damaged the Uffizi galleries.

LANDSCAPES

Tuscany is the region that, at least in terms of landscape, best represents Italy in its entirety, a region in which variety is united in a harmonious whole. It is rather a region of transition between the North and the South, but not for this one of mediation. It is rather a region that has always had its own identity; so much so that the phrase "Tuscan landscape" is used throughout the world to describe any place where, by some happy coincidence, there are rolling hills, knolls and valleys covered in lush greenery and possibly vineyards or olive groves. The hills that are central to the Tuscan landscape are perhaps, together with the coast, the area that has been most affected by the intervention of humans over the course of the centuries. Quite remarkably these interventions have actually "improved" on what could already have been described as perfection. Agriculture has found a place within the great natural scheme of things, exploiting every opportunity without altering the underlying structure. Even the earth-colored rural houses and the sinuous roads lined with cypresses are integral parts of the harmonious whole. Just as important in the topography of central Tuscany are the great villas. It would be impossible to compile here even a partial list of the noble estates that punctuate the countryside. The villas were usually built as a *buen retiro*, a place in which to escape from the city and political cares. But they were also symbols of

42 In the Chianti region the vineyards are the dominant feature of the landscape, adapting themselves to the terrain and occasionally allowing space for the residences of the landowners—top, a villa at Carmignano—or the rustic houses of the farmers.

43 The landscape of the Val d'Elsa cloaked in morning mist, as seen from the towers of San Gimignano: thus must have appeared the Tuscan countryside centuries ago.

the interest their owners nurtured in proper management of their agricultural land. The most well-known and celebrated area of Tuscany is probably the Chianti region set between the Arno and Ombrone rivers: a fairly small area but one that has become universally famous thanks to its wine. The vineyards of the Chianti—Sangiovese, Canaiolo nero, Malvasia and Trebbiano bianco grapes are combined to produce a ruby

44 High on a tufa upland, the village of Sorano is a mosaic of tall houses locked into one another in the typical medieval pattern. The 16th-century fortress is said to have been designed by Antonio Maria Lari.

red masterpiece—follow the contours of the hillsides. The Etruscans were the first people to cultivate vines in the area, thus initiating that morphological evolution that characterizes the Chianti hills. Subsequently, the monasteries continued their work, and the wealth of the area gave rise to that immense architectural patrimony that interrupts the regular agricultural patterns: blessed with the warm tones of the local stone, it includes farmhouses and castles, *pievi* and minute towns in which time appears to have stood still. History and geography have put the Chianti region between Florence and Siena, and art has placed a fundamental role in its definition. A town such as Certaldo, dominated by the red of the bricks, with its crenellated towers, its walls and silent alleys, could be taken as a paradigm of the towns of the region as a whole. So could San Gimignano, where architecture and nature are fused. A day in San Gimignano is probably one of the most emotional experiences a traveler could hope for: the village grew up on the Via Francigena, the most important medieval road. Wealthy thanks to trading along the route, San Gimignano eventually boasted 65 towers; just eight remain to remind us of past glories. But set out below those eight towers are the walls

45 top At Pitigliano the tufa is indistinguishable from the houses, a natural bastion that in the past made a significant contribution to the defense of the town. Having passed to the Orsini family, Pitigliano was classified as a city and enjoyed the prestige of bishopric. It was the powerful Tuscan family who equipped the town with fortifications designed by Antonio da Sangallo.

of the town, the Colle-giata di Santa Maria Assunta, the Piazza della Cisterna and great paintings and sculpture: frescoes by Taddeo di Bartolo, Benozzo Gozzoli and Barna da Siena, and two wooden statues by Jacopo della Quercia. In the Santa Fina Chapel there are veritable jewels of the art of Domenico Ghirlandaio and Benedetto da Maiano, enclosed in one of the most beautiful and representative examples of Tuscan Romanesque architecture. A perfect, self-contained miniature world that has remained intact since the 14th century. Not far away lies the province of Volterra, an area of unusual geological features set between the coastal region of Livorno and the Val d'Elsa. The provincial capital was one of the 12 Etruscan *lucumonie*—its importance is demonstrated by the size of the city walls dating from the 4th century BC. The city now lives on tourism and the working of the alabaster extracted

from the nearby quarries. In spite of its relative affluence, Volterra is faced by the threat of destruction: the *Balze*, or cliffs, on which it is built are subject to sudden subsidence that over the course of the centuries has swallowed necropoli and Etruscan remains and now endangers buildings such as the Badia Camoldese of San Giusto and San Clemente. The city manages to live with this threat, and it is perhaps its very precariousness that has saved it from speculation and rampant modernisation. Proceeding along the Via Francigena beyond Siena, one encounters another geological phenomenon, the Sienese *Crete*. These are the bleakest and most barren hills of the Valdelsa; they are known as the "Tuscan Desert" due to the yellow, gray, ocher and red coloring of the bare hilltops eroded by water that in places has excavated deep gorges. Among the fields of corn there are monuments of

46 top The gorges of the Balze around Volterra have over the course of the centuries swallowed necropoli, Etruscan walls and country houses. But they have also put a brake on the urban expansion of the town, thus preserving its medieval structure.

46 center The calanchi *reveal the red earth of the Sienese* Crete, *in the surroundings of Monte Oliveto.*

46 bottom Volterra, from its high spur of rock, dominates the surrounding countryside and the Balze (cliffs), as dramatic to the eye as they are dangerous to nearby buildings.

46-47 Volterra was one of the 12 Etruscan Lucumonie, and its importance is revealed by the dimensions of the ancient walls of which long stretches survive. Today the city lives principally on tourism and the working of alabaster.

48 left Early summer is a glorious season on the Sienese hills. The fields of grain are dotted with flowers and the crop is ripening, almost ready for the harvest and the beginning of a new cycle.

48 top and 48-49 The Sienese hills are proof that humankind can work in harmony with an extraordinarily beautiful landscape. One of the symbols of the Tuscan countryside are the cypresses that in addition to being decorative offer points of reference and provide particularly fine timber.

49 Isolated settlements, with houses set in the farmland, are a typical feature of the Sienese countryside. In this case it is likely to be the residence of a wealthy family as the estate has its own chapel.

incomparable beauty. Here medieval piety was responsible for the construction of some of most famous abbeys in Tuscany, including Monte Oliveto Maggiore immersed in a forest of holm oaks and cypresses and as robust as a fortress but softened by the frescoes of Luca Signorelli and Sodoma—splendor that contrasts with the highly evocative remains of the abbey of San Galgano, isolated in the valley of the Merse. Begun in the Gothic style in the 13th century, the abbey was a center of faith and culture for 200 years. Its decline set in early, however, and culminated with the collapse of its bell tower onto the roof. Abandoned and stripped of its precious fittings, today the church lies in ruins; what little remains is lovingly tended by a small community of nuns. A small community of French monks takes care of Sant'Antimo, the beautiful abbey in delicate roseate travertine and onyx close to Montalcino in the Val d'Orcia: attending the Sunday Mass and hearing the Gregorian chants that echo in the silence of the valley is a mystical experience. The medieval town of Montalcino is another center of the noble art of wine-making: it is here that the famous Brunello is produced, and each cellar claims to give life to the most precious bottles.

The beauty of the landscape and the stone-built villages of San Quirico, Bagni Visconti —with its great water-filled main square—and, above all Pienza, the ideal city designed by Rossellino for Pope Pius II, is sufficient in itself to satisfy the more abstemious visitors. Not faraway another architectural jewel, Montepulciano, lies between the Val d'Orcia and the Valdichiana. An aristocratic town, favored by its geographical position, Montepulciano is a compact summary of Tuscan art, influenced by both Florence and Siena. The high point is perhaps the pilgrimage church of the Madonna of San Biagio designed by Antonio Sangallo the Elder. Set outside the town, surrounded by cypresses, it is one of the most successful examples of the integration of sublime art and nature.

Yet another different landscape greets those who turn toward Monte Amiata, the gateway to the Maremma. The mountain was actually once an active volcano and seems almost out of place among the hills of the region. An almost perfect cone covered with woodland, for many years it was an important source of mercury. The surrounding villages contain memorials to Davide Lazzaretti, the "Christ of the Amiata," who was shot in 1878. You can climb

52 top The influence of both Florence and Rome made Montepulciano a city rich in Renaissance palazzi, thanks in part to the special status it was given by the Medici.

In this photo of the Palazzo Comunale, designed by Michelozzo in the 14th century, you can clearly see traces of the Palazzo della Signoria in Florence.

52-53 Set in the center of the mining area of the Grosseto Maremma, Massa Marittima features a medieval nucleus that converges on the irregular piazza in front of the Duomo, the Palazzo Pretorio and the Palazzo Comunale. The photo on the left shows the campanile of the Duomo.

53 top Still enclosed within its ancient walls, Cortona has preserved its Etruscan-Roman plan over which the medieval town developed.

53 bottom Colle Val d'Elsa is composed of two separate parts: Colle Alta, the higher town, has conserved its medieval appearance with important monumental buildings and the 13th-century city walls. Arnolfo di Cambio, famous sculptor and architect, is said to have been born in one of the tower houses.

Mount Labbro on foot to pay homage at the great cross erected in his honor; for your efforts you are rewarded with a 360-degree panoramic view across to the tufa towns of Sorano, Sovana and Pitigliano. The Maremma here is still green and rich in water and in the various villages Etruscan memories blend with those of noble families: the Orsini, local lords since 1503, left their mark and alongside the tufa houses rise imposing castles and massive fortifications. Not faraway, Saturnia, with its sulphurous spa waters and Etruscan connections, has become a sophisticated tourist destination set in an undulating landscape that becomes increasingly flat and barren. The classic Maremma ("wild country, an obscure route exposed the threat of bandits and thieves" wrote Giovanni Sercambi in the early 15th century) was for centuries one of the unhappiest areas of Tuscany, damned by malaria, enemy raids and chronic poverty. Paradoxically, in the Etruscan and Roman eras this was a flourishing region producing wine and olive oil, and the remains of the noble villas reveal their owners' devotion to their land. The abandonment and swamping of the coasts brought disease and misery, a situation that only began to change with the intervention of Peter Leopold in the second half of the 16th and beginning of the 17th century. Grosseto, the provincial capital, expanded at the expense of the ancient Roselle and is today a large town clustered around its substantial walls. The

Maremma has now been dominated by man: fields of grain, olive groves and herds of cattle guided by the *butteri,* the Tuscan cowboys who could have taught a thing or two even to Buffalo Bill. Descending toward the Tyrrhenian Sea, the Mediterranean maquis vegetation begins to dominate. The Parco dell'Uccellina, a dense green oasis, was founded in 1975 and is the result of human intervention. The reforesting of this marshy and completely abandoned area began under the Lorraine government: poplars, pines and cork oaks helped to stabilize the water table

54 top right Another moment in the lives of the Maremma butteri, *who concede little to modernity and much to tradition.*

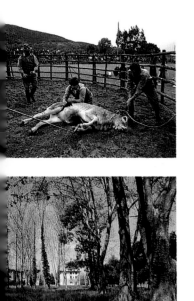

*54 top left
The Tournament of the Butteri sees the Maremma cowboys competing in various disciplines relating to cattle-herding. These are rough, crude events like the land in which they take place.*

*54 bottom left
The San Rossore estate, a few miles from Pisa, is a protected forest of three thousand hectares.
After having once belonged to the emperors, the bishops, the Medici and the Houses of Lorraine and Savoia, it is today part of the patrimony of the president of the Republic.*

and today the nature reserve provides secure breeding grounds for fallow deer, goats, otters, foxes, badgers and, of course, the wild boar, the symbol of the passion for hunting of the Maremma natives. Not far from the coast, Massa Marittima is another important Maremma town. The irregularly shaped piazza onto which the civic buildings face and the Romanesque cathedral are truly among the architectural treasures of Tuscany. Massa Marittima lies in the center of the Colline Metallifere, or the Metal Hills, which are rich in lead, copper, zinc, alum, pyrites and, above all, silver ore. The mines have created an unusual landscape; as ever, it was the Etruscans who first exploited the resources of the area and there are still signs of their activities, circular shafts in the vicinity in which foundries must have been located. Then, in the Middle Ages, a number of centers began to specialize in the working of metals and since then, with alternating fortune, the hills have continued to supply prime materials. Today many of the mines and quarries have become the target of industrial archaeologists. At Larderello the spectacle of the *soffioni* or, geothermal vents, provides a landscape that Dante might have described. In spite of being channelled and piped now, the *soffioni* still fill the air with clouds of white vapor. The area also boasts a wealth of Etruscan remains. Etruria never had a unified political and administrative configuration and

54-55 The Parco dell'Uccellina was, until the beginning of the last century, an area of marshes and scrub suitable only for hunting. Under the government of the House of Lorraine it was systematically re-forested and the water table was regulated. It is now a nature reserve.

55 The Monti dell'Uccellina housed, around the year 1000, Benedictine hermits who built their refuges in the wildest and most isolated areas. Of these only ruins remain, like those of the San Rabano Abbey.

56-57 The coastal pine forest of the Parco dell'Uccellina; below are the Canale dello Scoglietto and in the background, beyond the dunes, the Tyrrhenian Sea. The plantations of stone pines were first established by the House of Lorraine in the 18th century.

58-59 The flora and fauna of the Uccellina are typical of the Mediterranean maquis and the sandy coasts. The park attracts tourists prepared to respect nature and accept its rhythms: visitors may see goats, foxes, badgers or the kings of the Maremma, wild boar.

*60 top Another
corner of the
Garfagnana, one of
the greenest and most
densely forested areas
of Tuscany. Its
isolation was in the
past the source of
widespread legends
that were even
repeated by
historians, such as
Tito Livy, who wrote
"The women here are
as vigorous as men,
and the men as
ferocious as beasts."*

*60 center
The Apuan Alps have
supplied marble to
artists and builders
for over 2,000 years,
providing work and
a source of income for
the villages clinging
to the slopes. The
verdant valleys
contrast sharply with
the white of the
quarries.*

*60 bottom Capable
of extreme severity,
but also of sudden
softness, the
Garfagnana, set
between the Apuans
and the Tuscan-
Emilian Apennines,
is a territory still far
removed from
modern commotion.
This photo shows the
village of Turrite
Secca.*

*60-61 Colonnata in
the Apuan
Mountains, is one of
the Tuscan marble
capitals. Perched on
its mountaintop, it is
also celebrated for its
lard, said to be the
best in the world and
conserved in urns of
rough marble.*

this gave rise to several city-states. Among the most important were Vetulonia and Populonia. Of the grandeur of both only the faintest of traces remain, but they are sufficient to hint at past glories. Even though much of the devastation was caused by the negligence of humans, it is still an emotional experience to enter the burial mounds, or *edicola*, in which the ancient and mysterious civilization appears to rise again, solemn and silent. Both cities were in sight of the Tyrrhenian; the Tuscan coast is for the most part formed from the detritus brought down over the centuries by the Magra, Serchio, Arno, Cecina, Cornia, Bruna, Ombrone, Albenga and Flora rivers. This explains the sandy beaches separated by rocky spurs that represent a foretaste of the mountains just a few miles away as the crow flies. The other characteristic of the coast is its vegetation: the Mediterranean maquis is rich and varied, and the perfumes of arbutus, gum trees, juniper and mulberry blend with that of saltwater. And while many areas have been raped rather than merely touched by uncontrolled building and the need to provide holiday homes for the crowds of tourists, woods of holm, cork and bay oaks still resist. The dominant species is, however, the stone pine, which represents for the coastal region what the cypress represents for the inland hills, virtually a Tuscan trade-mark. The pines play a more than decorative role: they are an indispensable factor in protecting the inland areas from the salt air, a kind of natural green barrier separating the sea from the hills. The most intensively urbanized area of the coast is undoubtedly Versilia, which is now one long, uninterrupted paean to tourism. What at one time were individual fishing vil-

lages—Forte dei Marmi, Pietrasanta, Camaiore, Foccette and Viareggio— are now a jumbled sequence of bathing *stabilimenti*, hotels, villas and discotheques. Peace and tranquility can be found immediately inland, on the enchanting lake of Massaciuccoli, so dear to Giacomo Puccini, while drama is provided by the Apuan Alps, rising sharply toward the sky. Ever since ancient times, the Apuans have been famous for their marble quarries: the *statuario*, as white as snow, the light blue *bardiglio chiaro* and *bardiglio cupo*, the black and yellow *pavonazzo*, the green *cipollino*, the violet and orange *breccias*, the elegant *arabescato*, with gray veining. It was from here that

62 top Villa di Castello in the vicinity of Florence, once a Medici estate, today houses the Accademia della Crusca, responsible for the defense and diffusion of the Italian language. The garden, designed by Tribolo, features a fountain—seen in the top right—with a bronze group by Ammannati.

62-63 The Castello di Trebbio, between Barberino di Mugello and San Piero a Sieve, was constructed according to designs by Michelozzo. Today it is privately owned.

63 top Villa Mansi at Segromigno (not far from Lucca) dates back to the end of the 16th century, but was restored 200 years later by Filippo Juvara. It is one of the most famous villas in the Lucchese countryside and is surrounded by an English-style park and an Italianate garden overlooked by an airy loggia.

63 center The great frescoed reception hall of Villa Garzoni. The villa is at Collodi, the village close to Pescia famous for being the birthplace of Carlo Lorenzini, the author of Pinocchio.

63 bottom The Medici villa at Poggio a Caiano was constructed in the 15th century by Giuliano da Sangallo. The fashion for country retreats perhaps began with the Medici, who appreciated the possibility of spending a period of rest and relaxation away from the cares of the city. Soon, following their example, all the great families found it necessary to construct sumptuous country houses.

the marble used to build Augustus's Rome was quarried; Michelangelo came here in search of the right blocks for his masterpieces. Today, above all, it is the rich Arab sheikhs who commission palaces that recall the glories of the empire and the Renaissance. Beyond the Apuans, the Garfagnana provides yet another unforgettable landscape. Wild and isolated, cloaked with woodland—covering over 60 percent of the surface, almost a na-tional record—the Garfagnana is a kaleidoscope of gorges, valleys, villages and *pievi*. Within the Orecchiella National Park live deer, goats, mouflon and marmots. While Ludovico Ariosto may have cursed the destiny that brought him here, Giovanni Pascoli chose the Garfagnana as his refuge and last resting place. Before looking at the remaining mountains and the Tuscan islands, we should examine another area of importance in terms of history, culture and nature, the Lunigiana. The name of the area derives from Luni, even though the site now lies in Liguria by a matter of a few hundred yards. In Roman times it was an important town as here cargoes of marble were dispatched to the capital. The port then sank into the sea while the land, carried by the Magra, advanced. The highly evocative ruins reveal city walls and an amphitheater able to accommodate 6,000 spectators. Today the capitals of the marble trade are Massa and Carrara, friendly rivals with a common historical and political back-

ground. All that remains for Luni is the honor of having given its name to a region fundamental from a strategic point of view—Emilia is reached from here via the Cisa Pass. The museum at Pontremoli contains numerous examples of the mysterious stelae statues. The wooded mountain of Pistoia, crowned by the ski resort of Abetone, is the prelude to a landscape that once past the city is, unfortunately, highly industrialized: the fields have become greenhouses and the craft workshops are now factories. A welcome contrast is thankfully provided by the Mugello, the Casentino and Pratomagno. The Mugello, thanks to its benign geography and the political stability it enjoyed over the centuries, is a green valley with fertile terracing, olive groves, and woods of chestnut, holm oak and

64 top
The Argentario is an authentic natural paradise that has been saved from rampant speculative building. In spite of a lack of freshwater, the dominant color is green and vegetation covers the rocks that plunge into an uncontaminated sea.

beech. The tranquility of the area has always been a great attraction: the villa of Cafaggiolo at San Pietro a Sieve was an ancient fortress that in 1451 Michelozzolo transformed into a residence for the leisure pursuits of Cosimo the Elder, while at Pratolino Francesco dei Medici had a summer residence constructed for his beloved Bianca Capello. Fra Angelico was born at Vicchio, while close by at Vespignano Giotto first saw the light of day. The Casentino, to the north of Arezzo, is the region in which two great rivers, the Arno and the Tiber, both rise. Here again there are towns and villages and centers of religious piety such as Camaldoli Eremo, immersed in unspoiled forests. It was in 1012 that Romualdo and four companions chose the most isolated and silent spot in the Arno Valley in which to pray. The monastery, created as an outpost of the Eremo, achieved its fame and splendor in the 16th century, under the patronage of Lorenzo dei Medici—a member of the Accademia based here—and boasted a prestigious library. Just as suggestive is La Verna, where Saint Francis received the Stigmata.

The peace and serenity of the Casentino turn into bareness, surprise and mystery in the Pratomagno region, the long mountain ridge separating the valley from the Chianti hills. At one time there was a great lake here that gave rise to peculiar eroded rock formations. The *calanchi* emerge from the greenery surrounding the abbey of

64-65 *Facing Hidalgo Point, on the extreme tip of Punta Ala, is a handful of rocks scattered across the sea. The largest is known as the Scoglio dello Sparviero, or the Sparrow Hawk Rock; a ruined watchtower is perched on the summit.*

65 *top and center Punta Ala, an important yachting port and elite tourist resort, and Porto Ercole, which faces a natural bay overlooked by a castle and Spanish fortifications. The demands of modern tourism have led the small fishing village to become an elegant seaside resort clustered around the marina.*

65 *bottom Another view of the Argentario. These coasts were the object of major conflicts between France and Spain in the 16th century. Spain was the victor and created the Stato dei Presidi. There is still plenty of evidence of the occupation: fortifications dot the area, and ruined watchtowers can be found in the lush vegetation covering the rocks.*

Vallombrosa from where an almost lunar landscape can be admired. Descending toward Arezzo, at Loro Ciuffenna, is the lacustrine bowl that has proven to be a treasure house of fossils, with elephant, mastodon, hippopotami fossils plus examples of prehistoric flora found here now housed in the museum of palaeontology in Florence. From here you descend toward the Valdichiana: Arezzo is but one of the many unforgettable places. Rising once again toward the Val Tiberiana you reach San Sepolcro, the home town of Piero della Francesca and, further on, Monterchi, where you can admire his most tender and emotional fresco *Madonna del Parto*. To the south, on the other hand, is Cortona, situated on another ridge overlooking the nearby Lake Trasimeno, jewel of a Tuscan art city set in a verdant landscape.

Hills, mountains, plains and beaches, all that remain are the islands. Elba, Gorgona, Pianosa, Montecristo, Giglio and Giannutri, the Tuscan archipelago, were at one time peaks of the Western Alps as can be seen from a distance from the ferry out of Piombino. They rise from the sea steep and green. Their appeal was well known to the Etruscans who not only appreciated natural beauties but were astute enough to know how to exploit them. The iron ore deposits on Elba were also of interest to the Romans, but they preferred the leisure potential of the islands to the labors of mining. The excavations of the patrician villas are still underway, and each passing season reveals new wonders, usually situated in panoramic positions and equipped with comforts that would be the envy of modern vacationers. The archipelago is so beautiful that after the Romans had departed the islands were by no means left deserted. In fact, they attracted a series of would-be owners, including the Saracen pirates. Elba even became a miniature empire for Napoleon, and it was from here that his last, unsuccessful

venture began. The number of tourists visiting the island is now so great that measures are being taken to protect the environment with recycling programs, restricted use of water and detergents and increased use of bicycles rather than cars. The safeguarding of nature is an imperative at Montecristo, a closed reserve that is prohibited to all visitors after having been a penal colony and a hunting paradise for Vittorio Emanuele II. The other islands are caught between the desire to attract tourism and the need to preserve beaches, cliffs and vegetation. Pines, olives, cypresses, oaks, chestnuts, and a richly varied Mediterranean flora feeds and protects rare bird species, such as the peregrine falcon (on Gorgona and Giannutri), the shearwater (Capraia), migratory birds and a rare gull. Off Montecristo there are also occasional sightings of the monk seal. The islands are a surviving paradise to be defended at all costs in the name of the many areas of Italy ruined by negligence and greed.

68 top left Cala Rossa (top), on the island of Capraia, is hidden by the rocky point of the Zenobito (bottom). The other blood red rocky wall descends to the sea, creating an unusual contrast of colors. The coastline of Capraia is characterized by deep sea caves.

68 top right Giannutri is the southernmost of the Tuscan islands. The bay shown here takes its name from the Capel Rosso knoll, one of three knolls in the area. The others are Monte Mario and the Cannone knoll.

68 bottom right Cala dell'Allume, on the island of Giglio, is one of the most charming bays of the Tuscan archipelago. The island of Giglio owes its exceptionally mild climate to the density of the vegetation: ever since ancient times vineyards have been cultivated here, producing a distinctive wine, the Ansonaco. The local fauna also enjoys a particularly favorable environment—there are abundant wild rabbits, hares, partridges and woodcocks—and the seabed provides memorable excursions for divers.

68-69 The Roman's established a military base on Giannutri, the southernmost island of the Tuscan archipelago; there are numerous remains from the era and the seabed continues to throw up surprises for archaeologists.

69 top The gulls of Capraia. The island is the furthest from the coast (lying over 30 miles from the promontory of Piombino) and from a geological point of view it is of great interest as it is composed of slate, tufa, breccia and basalt: volcanic material, evidence of the archipelago's lively past.

70-71 The Fortezza di San Giorgio dominates a spur of rock on Capraia. Built by the Genoans, it rises almost 110 yards above the level of the sea, clinging to the rock that since ancient times has been the island's natural defense.

"When the going gets tough the Tuscans get going" would be an appropriate motto for the festivals, tournaments and popular celebrations that animate piazzas throughout the region. There is always a competitive edge, a desire to "put one over" on the opposition, perhaps to reclaim a symbolic trophy, or simply gain the respect and admiration of one's fellow citizens. That the Tuscans are a quarrelsome people is a cliché that has never really been forsworn; fortunately they now channel their aggression into their traditional sports. The beauty of their cities, their language and their sporting passion—in which winning is taken very seriously—are all to the benefit of the tourists crowding the squares during the major events. The vast majority of these spectacles have a long and glorious history or have been revived after a period of neglect. The exception to the rule is the Viareggio Carnival, a money-spinning pageant of allegorical floats that has more in common with the world of business (and the national lotteries) than with folklore. Elsewhere the competitive spirit is still that of the Middle Ages, perhaps tamed somewhat and modified according to the tastes of the Renaissance, when even popular enthusiasm had to have a certain class. Aggression rarely

72-73 The Calcio Storico *is played on the square in front of Santa Croce in June. The games were originally played in late January, and in 1530 were actually held on the frozen Arno. But not only are the competitors more eager to fight it out in the summer, but there are also considerably more tourists. Nevertheless, the sport remains one of the most deeply and intimately Florentine of events, linked as it is to the four historic quarters of the city. The rules of the* Calcio Storico *are complex and the number of players on the field—27 per team—makes life difficult for the referees. Scuffles are the order of the day, as are the destruction of the beautiful colored costumes, bruises and creative vernacular insults. At the end the winning quarter takes home a calf to be roasted and eaten during the great concluding celebrations.*

74 top left Lucca, like many other Tuscan cities, has a very strong tournament tradition. This illustration shows the gigantic crossbows that require not only skill but also considerable physical strength.

74 bottom left The Giostra del Saracino in Arezzo. The knights have to try to strike the mannequin representing the Saracen while avoiding his whip, which is loaded with lead weights.

spills over into violence if, that is to say, one ignores the invective and the highly colored cursing that accompanies each and every event and that is frequently amusing and imaginative rather than brutal. Most cities have their own particular sport. In Florence the *sferomachia*, as the *Crusca Dictionary* elegantly defines it, degenerates into the dustiest and most chaotic of football matches imaginable. As Lewis Carroll's Alice might say, "They play without rules, and if there are rules, they ignore them." Four teams represent the four city quarters and the four natural elements (San Giovanni, as the land in green, Santa Croce as water in blue, Santa Maria Novella as fire in red and Santo Spirito as the air in white); there are 27 players on the field for each team, together with a referee (the "Maestro di Campo"), who frequently does not know to which saint he should turn. The spectacle is completed by an extremely complicated set of rules that perhaps only the Florentines themselves really understand, the incitement of the spectators (who at crucial moments do not hesitate to descend from the stands in support of their team) and a pledge of sportsmanship that would appear to be written on the waters of the Arno—soon sworn and even sooner forgotten. At the end of the tournament held in June in Piazza Santa Croce, and preceded by a flag twirling competition, the players are bruised and battered, their beautiful tunics are torn to shreds and the victors celebrate by eating the prize, a white calf. As ever, the losers start planning their revenge. At Pistoia the sport acquires a more noble tone and

takes the form of a competition of skill rather than brute force. The *Giostra dell'Orso*, the Bear Joust, held in July in honor of Saint James, dates way back: at one time it was the *Palio dei Barbieri*, a breakneck race involving the entire city and preceded by violent games on the borderline of legality. Five hundred years later the revived event has become more civilized. In Piazza Duomo, the 12 horsemen representing the various city parishes attempt to strike a target in the shape of a bear—the symbol of the city of Pistoia—with the tips of their lances. Again the main event is set off

74 right On the first Sunday in September Arezzo echoes to the sound of drums and trumpets announcing the herald, who reads the proclamation of the Giostra del Saracino. In the afternoon the weapons of the competitors are blessed in front of the local parish churches, and after a parade the tournament begins in Piazza Grande.

75 The origins of the Giostra del Saracino held in Arezzo date back to the 12th century. The knights "running the lance" represent the quarters of Porta Sant'Andrea, Porta Crucifera, Porta del Foro and Porta Santo Spirito.

by characters in 15th-century dress, drummers, flag twirlers, dames and knights. Historical revival is also the name of the game at Arezzo with the *Giostra del Saracino*, the Saracen Joust. This event celebrates the knightly tournaments of the Middles Ages held to mark the arrival in the city of important personages and in which the local gentlemen competed for the usual *palio* or banner. Today the competitors are representatives of the city quarters and enact the joust in the main square, Piazza Grande. The target is a marionette, a dummy representing the hated Saracen and capable of extracting his own revenge by striking an inexpert knight with a whip of weighted balls. A regatta on the waters of the Arno is the main attraction of Pisa's Saint Ranieri celebrations held between the 16th and the 17th of July. During the night thousands of oil lamps are lit along the riverbanks, on the balconies of the buildings (together with the *biancheria*, a white wooden support) and on miniature boats. With all other illumination extinguished the river glows like a long tongue of fire descending slowly toward the sea. The following day the city's valiant oarsmen evoke the era in which Pisa contended control of the Mediterranean with Venice, Genoa and Amalfi in the *Regata delle Repubbliche Marinare*.

76 left The Regatta of the Marine Republics at Pisa is a riot of sumptuous costumes—like that of the doge with his ermine cloak and of the young lady—and competitive spirit, with teams from Pisa, Venice, Genoa and Amalfi engaged on the waters of the Arno.

76 right The detonation of the wagon on Easter morning in front of the Duomo reveals the fortunes of the coming year for the Florentines. The powder is ignited by the "dove," a rocket that departs from the high altar in the cathedral.

77 The Regatta of the Marine Republics attracts thousands of spectators to Pisa, but the lights of San Ranieri illuminate the city's most heart-felt festival. During the night of June 16, the street lamps are switched off and small oil lamps trace the outlines of the building and the banks of the river. As dusk falls thousands of little boats carrying lamps are launched toward the sea.

The sea again figures strongly in the *Palio Marinaro* at Livorno, while the citizens of Sansepolcro re-enact the *Palio delle Balestre*, another event with medieval roots. However, the greatest and the most famous of these sporting occasions is undoubtedly the *Palio* held in Siena. The thousands of tourists crowding the Piazza del Campo and the millions of television spectators see but the briefest of races around the square, a kaleidoscope of galloping horses, nervous jockeys and feverishly excited *contradaioli,* or local supporters. For anybody born beyond the shadow of the Mangia Tower it must be very difficult to comprehend exactly what lies behind the apparently straightforward event: months and months of preparations, discussions, arguments and reconciliation, rivers of money that pass from hand to hand, miles of colored cloth, curses and blessings, banquets and secret negotiations, friendships broken and alliances sealed. The animal rights activists protest, hopelessly pleading for the suppression of a sport in which the horse is the undisputed king. They cry over the poor beasts injured on the San Martino Curve, but not a tear is shed for the jockeys who if they fall are lucky to be treated. Their mounts, on the other hand, are more cosseted— spoiled, tamed and fed with love—than

78 Thousands of pages have been written about the Palio of Siena, and yet for those born beyond the shadow of the Mangia Tower it is difficult to comprehend the passion and fervor of the Sienese for this competition.
At the top, the banner of the Selva; below, the blessing of the horse of one of the contrade *in the parish church.*

78-79 and 79 top This wagon, drawn by four oxen, carries the Palio banner: it is a stirring moment in which every self-respecting Sienese citizen is already anticipating the honor of being a member of the victorious contrada. In the large photo, a contrada member proudly bearing the banner of "his" Tartuca.

79 right During the day of the race, even the contrade that are not taking part in the Palio have their moment of glory. This photo shows a member of the Contrada del Gallo.

the most fortunate of crown princes. A veterinary surgeon is more esteemed than any professor of human medicine and at the end of their careers the heroic steeds' final destination is not the abattoir but comfortable farms on the Sienese hills. As pampered pensioners, they possibly recall the days in which the place of honor, in church as well as at the banqueting table, was reserved for them. In their mind's eye they will may still see the colors of the *contrada* they carried to victory or the pennant dedicated to the Madonna that their feats conquered. The Tuscan taste for celebration manifests itself not only in the major tournaments; in Florence, for example, Easter would hardly be Easter without the *Scoppio del Carro*, an ancient propitiatory ceremony (dating back to the first Crusade): the detonation of the dove that sets off the fireworks in the wagon in front of the Duomo is a source of interminable discussion. A whole-hearted explosion announces a happy and prosperous year, while a damp squib augurs a sad and ill-favored time for all. In September the Virgin's birthday is marked by the *Festa delle Rificolone*—crepe paper lanterns illuminate the San Nicolò Bridge while boats descend the Arno. Other festivals celebrate local produce such as the ones at Impruneta or Colonnata. In terms of the delights of the palate, no visit to Tuscany would be complete without sampling some of the local delicacies. The fertility of the countryside and a gastronomic tradition based on the excellence of its natural

81 During the race
friendships and
family ties go by the
boards in the name
of competition.
Occasionally
corruption raises its
ugly head: it is not
unknown for a
contrada to "buy off"
the jockey of one of its
rivals. All's fair in
love, war and the
Palio of Siena.

82-83 The San
Martino corner
rounded during the
Palio at Siena is
rightly feared by even
the most expert and
audacious of jockeys.
It is here that the most
spectacular and
dangerous falls occur,
dangerous for both the
horses and their riders.
The padding intended
to provide protection
is of little help.

ingredients have given rise to some flavorsome cooking. Olive oil takes pride of place and a slice of *panunto* (seasoned bread), flavored with garlic is one of the tastiest of foods one could find. The Chianina cattle provide the renowned *Fiorentine*, thick T-bone steaks to be cooked on charcoal grills, while the heights of fish cuisine are reached with the *caciucco*, from Livorno. Then there are various kinds of sheep's cheese: the *pecorino* from Siena, the *ravaggiolo* of the Mugello and the *marzolino*. These should all be washed down with a glass

of Tuscan wine, Brunello from Montalcino, Vin Nobile from Montepulciano, Vernaccia from San Gimignano, or Chianti, perhaps the world's most famous wine. The name "Chianti" derives from the Etruscan *Clante-i* and was originally used to identify a product of high quality. In 1924 a consortium was set up to protect the identity and character of the wine of the Chianti region and restrict the use of its symbol, a black cockerel on a gold background. As early as the late 19th century, however, Bettino Ricasoli, the father of the Chianti wine culture, had established the parameters for identifying the real McCoy: seven tenths Sangiovese (body and color), two tenths Canaiolo (bouquet and smoothness) and a tenth of Trebbiano and Malvasia (acidity and refinement). It is still a winning recipe, in spite of attempts at imitation so numerous that Harold Acton was to say that if all the wine sold as Chianti was produced in the region, then the Chianti hills would have to extend as far as the steppes of Central Asia.

The countryside has also nurtured a rich craft tradition that has to some extent resisted encroaching industrialization. Leather, paper and wickerwork are still produced in Florence, and the city also supports a flourishing restoration trade. In the region of Volterra alabaster is the prime material for statues, while on the Apuan hills marble is worked. At Scarperia in the Mugello the art of the knife makers is alive and well. The trade has ancient origins and in 1538 was regulated by a statute. Then there are the antique fairs like those of Arezzo and Cortona, justly famous throughout the world.

THE CITIES

FLORENCE

From the Roman *castrum* to the city of today: historical and artistic developments have led to Florence becoming an immensely complex urban center that is by no means easy to manage, so much so that each and every innovation is greeted with interminable argument. The Roman city plan (the *cardo* corresponds to the modern-day Via degli Speziali and Via Strozzi, and the *decumano* to the junction of Vias Roma and Calimala) was overlaid with an extremely random and varied medieval structure, while this itself has been altered by the Renaissance structures and the demolition work of the last century performed in the name of a so-called restoration of the city center. The result is that today those who arrive in Florence expecting to find a great open-air museum will instead find a living, breathing and mutating city, as is only right and proper. The regional capital of Tuscany has been spared, at least in part, the sad fate of Venice, which is paying for its status as an artistic jewel in terms of a shrinking, aging population. Prisoners of the tourists, the Venetians are gradually surrendering to the inevitable, crossing Ponte della Libertà and settling in exile in Mestre. Under siege, but resolute, the Florentines are putting up

86-87 The center of Florence, dominated by the dome of Santa Maria del Fiore and the smaller one of San Lorenzo. Behind the curtain of buildings marking the course of the Arno can be seen the medieval street plan of the city.

87 top Ponte Vecchio, Ponte Santa Trinità and Ponte alla Carraia follow one after the other over the waters of the Arno. Miraculously spared the destruction of the Second World War, the Ponte Vecchio today houses famous jewelers' shops but was once the city's meat market.

87 right Probably begun according to designs by Arnolfo di Cambio in 1294 and completed in the last century with a mediocre "historical" facade, Santa Croce is the pantheon of the national heroes; here are buried Alfieri, Machiavelli, Michelangelo, Vasari, Rossini and Ugo Foscolo, who in his poem Sepolcri, *sang the praises of the inspiration behind the church.*

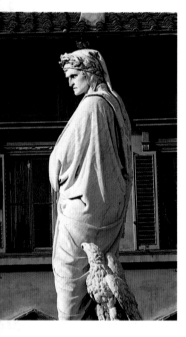

88 left
The monument to Dante, perhaps the most famous Florentine citizen, by Enrico Pazzi in Piazza Santa Croce. The square has housed, since ancient times, great crowds, some to hear the preaching of Saint Bernardino of Siena, others attracted by various games and tournaments.

strenuous resistance: they may have ceded the city center to fast food and pizza joints but they refuse to allow intrusions into their daily lives. Walk through one of the street markets and you will still hear the distinctive local speech patterns. Pass an evening at the Pergola theater or one of the local nightclubs and you will realize that the tourists have yet to conquer this particular city. In the Florentine workshops authentic artisans work not for the passing Americans happy to pick up an industrial reproduction of a Renaissance *putto*, but for the great families restoring the palazzi of their forebears piece by piece. The scholars at the National Library, the Laurenziana and Mediceo-Ricciardiana Library, at the Marucelliana, at the Viesseux and at the Accademia della Crusca are working for the benefit of Italian culture, certainly not for the benefit of the all-inclusive tour visits. The *Opificio delle Pietre Dure* does not sell lapis lazuli necklaces, but restores precious objects. This all goes to show that you cannot expect to visit Florence for a couple of days of ritual sightseeing and leave thinking that you have done it all. You could hardly say you know New York without having walked in Central Park or that you know Paris without ever having dined in a bistro. Similarly Florence should be seen as a proud and vital city refusing to live on its past laurels and determined to continue its thousand-year development, to the chagrin of those who would prefer to see it placed in a glass museum case.

88 top right Built by Michelozzo in the middle of the 15th century, the Palazzo Medici-Riccardi today houses the prefecture. The courtyard contains Bandinelli's statue of Orpheus, set off by the beguiling perspective of the arcades.

88 center right The Florentine lily, symbol of the city council since the time of the Medici, appears on the pediment over the entrance to the Palazzo Vecchio.

88 bottom right Created according to the wishes of Eleonora, the wife of Cosimo I, the Boboli Gardens mirror late Renaissance taste, with grottoes, walks, fountains, vast lawns and clipped hedges. This photo shows Neptune's Pool.

89 Piazza della Signoria is graced by a wealth of sculpture. In the foreground is Baccio Bandinelli's Hercules and Cacus; then comes the copy of Michelangelo's David and, in the background, Ammannati's Neptune Fountain. A circle in front of the fountain marks the spot where Savonarola was hanged and set on fire.

90 At dusk two of the symbols of Florence stand out, the Palazzo della Signoria and the church of Santo Spirito. The last fruit of the genius of Brunelleschi, Santo Spirito displays an austere and unusually simple facade. The dome and the campanile were added at later dates.

91-94 Ponte Vecchio seems like a veritable city, an agglomeration of buildings stacked up on the ancient spans. Today it is famous for its jewelers' shops, but it was once the realm of the Florentine butchers.

95 *The bulk of the Duomo of Florence emerges against the city skyline. The audacity of Brunelleschi's dome, a masterpiece of stability and lightness, stunned the artist's contemporaries. It sits alongside Giotto's Tower which, with its perfect proportions, is further evidence of the genius of Angelo di Bondone, the shepherd turned artist.*

96 In the midst of the uniform street plan of Siena, miraculously intact after-so many centuries, rises the great bulk of the Duomo with, in the background, the red brick bowl of the Piazza del Campo.

Sealed as it is within its city walls, and set in one of the most beautiful landscapes in the world, Siena has had the privilege of maintaining intact its original appearance. It is at night, when the shops are closed and the illuminated signs are switched off that wandering the arched streets, you appreciate the unique qualities of the city. Privilege has its price of course: it is difficult to adapt to modern life when every stone is a part of history. The original nucleus, perched on three hills that meet at the Croce del Travaglio, has been influenced by the morphology of the landscape, and even Pizza del Campo owes its inclination to the natural slope: a broad terra-cotta red bowl amidst a labyrinth of streets in which

openings are rare due to the need to utilize space to the best effect while remaining as far as possible within the beloved city walls. Siena continues to enjoy a degree of isolation; reaching the city by train, for example, is an enterprise best left to the most patient of travelers. The highway linking it to Florence passes through an area of rare beauty and plugs it into the national motorway network, but it has to be said that much of the appeal of the city lies in its remaining tranquil and a little disdainful, with that civic pride that the knocks of contemporary life have failed to dent.

97 bottom left The shadow of the Mangia Tower is traced on the buildings and the pavement of the Piazza del Campo. The elegant noble palazzi that surround the piazza were built according to severe norms established by the council at the end of the 13th century to preserve the dignity of the city's showpiece square.

97 top right The 14th-century Palazzo Salimbeni, the home of the Monte dei Paschi di Siena bank, has a Gothic Revival appearance thanks to the 19th-century modifications made by Giuseppe Partini.

97 bottom right The color of the houses and the roofs of Siena is warm and homogeneous; it recalls the tones of the Crete, the surrounding countryside, in a perfect fusion of art and nature.

98 top Seen from the walls of Lucca, the garden of the Palazzo Pfanner shows the elaborate taste of the 17th century. The palazzo now houses a costume museum.

98-99 Piazza del Mercato, one of Lucca's best-loved squares, cannot hide its origins: during Roman times it was the site of the amphitheater and it has preserved its perfect oval plan. To the right runs the Fillungo, a long street that almost bisects the historic town center.

LUCCA

The origins of Lucca are mysterious. The Celtic-Ligurian derivation of its name indicates that it may be pre-Roman. *Luk* was the term used to describe a marshy area and, in fact, at one time there was the ancient Lake of Bientina in the area that occasionally flooded the surrounding countryside. Today, on the other hand, Lucca is one of the most pleasant Italian cities in which to live, not only for the beauty of its palazzi and churches, the urbanity of its compact and harmonious city center and its truly human dimensions, but also for the extraordinary setting in which it lies. The Luccesian countryside, with its hills of vineyards and olive groves punctuated by lavish villas, is the perfect counterpoint to the provincial capital itself. It is as open as Lucca is closed inside its massive walls and bastions; as dedicated to leisure as Lucca is industrious and founded, from the earliest times, on a solid mercantile class. The solidity of wool and silk did not impede Lucca from acquiring a feminine quality, tied as it is to the angelic face of Ilaria del Carretto, wife of Paolo Guinigi, who rests in the Duomo of San Martino portrayed by Jacopo della Quercia in one of the most serene and "affectionate" works in the history of art. Ilaria and the beauty of love is at the heart of any visit to Lucca.

99 Piazza San Michele in Foro is one of the key squares in Lucca. More central than the Duomo, with its imposing facade crowned by the statue of the archangel, the San Michele church was built on the foundations of an 8th-century temple.

PISA

Ligurians, Ionians and Etruscans all have claims on the founding of Pisa. However, even though today the city is to be found some miles from the coast, the sea is its true raison d'être. Between the years 1000 and 1300 the development of its maritime power was quite remarkable. The Pisans fought against the Saracens, they participated in the Crusades and conquered Sardinia, Corsica and Majorca. And at the same time they transformed their city into a work of art. Today the ancient battles have been forgotten. The city does, however, retain its cultural position: the Pisan university is one of the oldest in Italy, with a supremacy recognised in Roman law. The Scuola Normale Superiore, founded by Napoleon and reorganized by Leopold II in 1846, is a point of departure—or arrival—for the most brilliant minds in the country. The University of Pisa has attracted Alfieri, Leopardi, Byron, Shelley and Elizabeth Barret Browning and embodies a strongly rooted cultural tradition nurtured under the protective wing of Galileo Galilei, to whom modern physics owes the scientific method of investigation still used today that integrates the results of experiments and observations and is fundamental in the formulation of theories. This method might well have had its origins in the very heart of the city, below the great bronze incense lamp hanging in the Duomo, Galileo's lamp.

100 top left The small church of Santa Maria della Spina on the banks of the Arno derives its name from a relic of Christ's Crown of Thorns now in the church of Santa Chiara. Pinnacles, niches, cusps and arcades make it a jewel of Gothic architecture.

100 bottom left Pisa and the Arno seen from the Torre dell'Orologio. The banks of the Arno at Pisa, lined by sober palazzi, are illuminated during the San Ranieri celebrations when every balcony is decorated with a line of small lamps.

100 right The statue of Cosimo I in Piazza dei Cavalieri, the heart of the ancient republican city. Palazzo dei Cavalieri, rebuilt by Giorgio Vasari for the Order of Saint Stephen, is the home of the Scuola Normale Superiore.

101 The Piazza dei Miracoli complex at Pisa—the Baptistery, the Duomo, the Tower and the Camposanto—is a monument dedicated to God, but also a memorial to the wealth achieved by the city thanks to maritime trading, the expeditions to the Middle East and North Africa and its victories over the infidels and its business rivals.

There are four Tuscan Queens, Florence, Pisa, Siena and Lucca. But the ladies-in-waiting are no less worthy of love, consideration and respect. One by one virtually all of the cities in the region have played leading roles in political and artistic events, but history has called on just a few of them to emerge leaving the others in an aura of tranquility that has nothing in common with mediocrity. Taken one by one, Livorno, Grosseto, Massa, Carrara, Arezzo and Pistoia have nothing to fear in comparison with other artistic centers, not only in Italy, but throughout the world. Each of these living cities has certain distinguishing characteristics: at Livorno it is the sea; at Grosseto it is the Maremma and the Etruscan civilization; Massa and Carrara are the undisputed capitals of the marble industry; Arezzo is the center of the goldsmiths' trade; and Pistoia is the capital of one of the wealthiest and most industrialized areas of Tuscany. If they do have to follow a half step behind the four queens, they nevertheless maintain their noble status with pride, frequently in close contact with the extraordinarily varied surrounding countryside in which each church, each house and each farm has its own history and is ready to recount it.

102 top left Piazza Dante is the heart of Grosseto, enclosed within its massive walls. In the center is a statue of Leopold II erected in recognition of the grand duke's efforts to control malaria, a disease endemic to the Maremma. In the background is the Palazzo della Provincia.

102 bottom left The sumptuous Palazzo Cybo Malaspina at Massa, decorated with 18th-century white stucco. The palazzo is in Piazza Aranci, which takes its name from the orange trees lending it shade.

102-103 The Canale della Fortezza Nuova constitutes the so-called "New Venice," a 17th-century quarter with buildings destined for sailors and fishermen. Proceeding along the canal one reaches the Fortezza Vecchia, built by Antonio da Sangallo the Younger in the first half of the 16th century.

103 top Piazza Grande at Arezzo, surrounded by buildings that summarize the history of the city, from the Palazzo del Tribunale to that of the Fraternità dei Laici and the Logge by Giorgio Vasari.

103 top right Carrara—in this photo a palazzo on Piazza Alberica—is the world marble capital. The city's quarries supply the brilliant white statuario, Michelangelo's favorite material. Behind the city rise the Apuan Alps, where the landscape appears to be covered in snow thanks to the quarries.

103 bottom right The portico of the Ospedale del Ceppo at Pistoia is decorated with a polychrome terra-cotta frieze from the Della Robbia studio; it illustrates the seven works of mercy.

The most recent research into Etruscan art has led to two fundamental considerations: first, that it cannot be considered as having unitary, homogeneous characteristics, and second, that it is an artistic phenomenon owing much to the Hellenistic tradition. It was principally the cities of southern Etruria—those that are for the most part to be found in the Lazio region today—that enjoyed a political and cultural hegemony; the monumental tombs of Cerveteri are convincing proof of that fact. The art of painting developed at Tarquinia, while Vulci specialized in ceramics and Veio in sculpture. The influence of this series of art and craft specializations reached as far North as Volterra and Fiesole. This was in the 7th century BC, a period in which the Hellenic influence was extremely strong as Greek artists were employed by the leading figures of the Etruscan cities, anxious to perpetuate their family histories. It was a period of great splendor that only began to show signs of decline in the difficult political atmosphere of the 5th century.

During the 4th century a degree of revival led to the establishment of other artistic schools: decorators of alabaster urns at Volterra and of ceramic urns in other large and small cities. Etruscan ceramics are worthy of more detailed discussion. *Bucchero* was typical of Cerveteri, where vases and urns were produced with very thin walls and decoration of clearly Greek derivation. Ceramic production spread through-

104 top Famous throughout the world, The Wounded Chimera of Bellerofonte, *also known as the* Arezzo Chimera, *dates back to the 5th century* BC. *Discovered in 1555, it was restored by Benvenuto Cellini. In the Etruscan era Arezzo was an important center for bronze work.*

104 bottom The slim Etruscan statuettes found at Brolio in the Val di Chiana represent a warrior and a lady; they presumably date back to around 550 BC *and probably served as supports for a piece of wooden furniture.*

out the region and the influence of foreign artists allowed extremely high-quality objects to be produced. The ceramic artists were not, however, well-known figures (with the exception of Aristonoto), but paid craftsmen, generally employed to reproduce the established, traditional stylistic motifs that appealed to an aristocracy eager to seal their place in history. This situation created the conditions for the formation of other centers of specialization: funerary architecture at Cerveteri, monumental painting at Tarquinia and sculpture at Vulci. The Guarnacci Etruscan Museum at Volterra provides a useful overview of the art of this mysterious civilization. The museum contains the funerary trappings found in the numerous necropoli of the region: around 700 tufa, terra-cotta and alabaster urns, including the well-known example with decorative elements depicting a couple of presumed newlyweds. There are also stelae celebrating warlike virtues and cinerary urns from the Villanovian era. Jewelry, coins and small bronzes are testimony to the variety of influences and styles that combined in this fascinating period of artistic expression. The Archaeological Museum at Arezzo is equally interesting and contains a number of Roman exhibits and finds from the tombs around Populonia, Vetulonia and Sovana. The "Romanization" of Tuscia was rapid and extensive, although evidence of the republican and imperial splendors were frequently covered by and incorporated into the

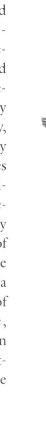

105 top A bust of the young Augustus conserved in the Guarnacci Etruscan Museum at Volterra. Even though political events had put the city in danger on several occasions, in the era of Imperial Rome Volterra continued to enjoy a full cultural life. The construction of the Roman theater dates from this period.

105 bottom The sarcophagus of Larthia in polychrome terra-cotta discovered at Chiusi and conserved in the Archaeological Museum in Florence. This museum, housed in the Palazzo della Crocetta, is one of the most important of its kind and also features Greek and Roman sculpture and Egyptian and numismatic sections.

medieval cities. The archaeological digs at Fiesole brought to light a large Roman theater and remains of thermal baths from the 1st century AD, and there are also traces of large monumental complexes at Volterra and Roselle. In the latter case there are remains of the city walls, the forum, noble houses, thermal baths and an amphitheater, evidence of a wealthy and glorious past. On the island of Elba excavations are still underway to bring to light Roman villas decorated with precious mosaics while the Maremma conceals, amidst its Etruscan remains, sumptuous noble residences. Perhaps the most evocative reminder of the epoch is to be found in the center of Lucca, in the beautiful Piazza Anfiteatro whose oval form has been respected by the constructions of successive eras and in which traces of the tribunes can still be seen: a perfect example of architectural integration. It was in the Middle Ages that Tuscany assumed a pivotal role in the history of Italian art. The phenomenon is all the more interesting in that it involved not only the major cities, such as Florence, Lucca, Siena and Pisa, but also the smaller centers. Almost perfectly intact medieval towns such as San Gimignano and Monteriggioni are clear evidence of this fact. The dominant art form was architecture with differing stylistic elements from one area to the next and various influences being imported from France and Lombardy. In the case of the church of San Miniato al Monte in Florence, the Florentine Romanesque style has clearly been influenced by early Christian motifs, with the luminous facade in white-and-green marble anticipating the geometrical rigor of much of the art of the city. Equally characteristic are San Giovanni, the baptistery mentioned by Dante, with its severe austerity and the Badia Fiesolana. Emphasized by the green-and-white Prato marble, massive yet at the same time airy with its pyramidal roof, the Baptistery at Florence has been enriched over the centuries with innumerable works of art. The magnificent bronze doors, the fruit of the genius of Andrea Pisano (the south door) and Lorenzo Ghiberti (the doors to the north and the west, the "Gates of Paradise," according to Michelangelo), the 13th-century mosaics and the *Christ* by Coppo di Marcovaldo are all set in a relatively compact space and represent a summation of Florentine art.

107 left Poppi, in the Casentino, is celebrated for its Palazzo Pretorio, once the castle of the Guidi Counts. It houses an important library, the strict custodian of manuscripts, incunabula and rare books.

107 top right San Miniato al Monte is considered to be the most beautiful example of the Florentine Romanesque. The facade, with its white-and-green marble, stands tall and luminous on Monte delle Croci and is visible from much of the city.

107 bottom right The Badia Fiesolana, the origins of which lie prior to the year 1000, has preserved its original facade with the typical two-color geometric decorations. Alongside is the former convent housing the European University.

108 left Tradition attributes the construction of the campanile of the Duomo of Pisa to Bonanno. The tower was originally designed to be much taller, but subsidence halted building work for almost a century and then restricted the overall height.

108 top The apse in the Duomo at Pisa is, like the facade, by Rainaldo, who continued the work of Buscheto. The architect is remembered in an inscription at the base of the first order on the facade; he is defined as a prudens operator et ipse magister *(brilliant architect and master).*

108-109 The facade of the Duomo is considered to be the model for an architectural genre. The motif of the superimposed loggias is Lombard in origin, but Rainaldo enriched it with intricate intaglio work, cornices and inlay decoration.

The other major Romanesque thread in Tuscany is to be found at Pisa and Lucca and involves the development of Lombard themes, revised with supreme elegance and the addition of Arabic motifs. The latter were the fruit, in the case of Pisa, of the city's maritime connections. Buscheto, the architect of the first version of the Duomo at Pisa at the end of the 11th century, took on the classical inheritance and reinterpreted it, setting the tone for a number of other buildings, such as the churches of San Frediano and Sant'Alessandro at Lucca. Pisa's Campo dei Miracoli can be said to be the archetype of Pisan Romanesque architecture in spite of having been constructed in different periods and with the contribution of various artists. During the Longobard era Lucca had enjoyed the privilege of being the ducal seat and the capital of the region, a period of great splendor. Shortly after the year 1000, early in the era of the free communes, it was the setting for some of Tuscany's most beautiful Romanesque architecture, rivaled only by that of Pisa. The codified forms of Buscheto were simplified: San Martino, San Michele and Sant'Alessandro have a coherence and severity barely disturbed by decoration. Subsequent buildings saw an increasing use of chromatism and toward the middle of the 12th century new facades began to be applied to the oldest churches. Lucca is also notable for its country churches, the *pievi* of Gattaiola, Santa Maria del Giudice and Loppia, monuments to popular piety. The Romanesque style

110 top left Set close to the San Colombano bastion, San Martino, the Duomo of Lucca, was perhaps founded by San Frediano in the 6th century, but the building we know today dates back to the 11th through the 13th centuries. It contains one of the world's most beautiful works of art, the tomb of Ilaria del Carretto by Jacopo della Quercia.

110 bottom The mosaic high on the facade of San Frediano at Lucca is attributed to the pupils of Berlinghieri. It depicts the Ascension of Christ and in spite of the heavy-handed restoration of the last century, it retains the plasticity and coloring typical of the Lucchese masters.

was also a feature of the architecture of Pistoia, with a distinct local variation seen in monuments such as the Duomo, Sant'Andrea, San Bartolomeo in Pantano, San Giovanni Fuorcivitas and San Pietro as well as many minor churches in the city and the surrounding countryside. Sacred architecture was complemented and supported by the flourishing art of sculpture, itself influenced by French Gothic and the rich Lombard tradition. With the work of Bonanno (the doors of the Duomo at Pisa, the sculptures of the Duomo at Lucca and the *pievi* of Arezzo and Pistoia), Gugliemo, Gruamonte and Biduino—who left traces of his art above all at Lucca—the ground was prepared for the greatest sculptor of the 13th century, Nicola Pisano. Coming from Puglia and the Federician court and having a classical background, Pisano rejected once and for all the Byzantine tradition, inventing a brand new sculptural language that laid the basis for a more human and heroic art form. The pulpit in the baptistery at

110 top right The church of San Michele at Lucca dates from the late Lucchese Romanesque period, plastic, solemn, yet extremely light. The luminosity of the marble is also found in the campanile and contrasts with the severe atmosphere of the interior.

110 center right Another view of the Duomo of Lucca: this shot reveals the richness of the apse and the complexity of the structure.

111 The Duomo of Pistoia has extremely ancient origins; it was rebuilt in the 12th century and in the 14th century a portico was added to the facade. The campanile was originally a Longobard watchtower and in the late 13th century was transformed with the construction of the three final loggias in the Pisan Romanesque style.

Pisa is a truly a fundamental work in the history of Italian art: Pisano drew on models from ancient sculpture, discovering a certain dignity and culture that were eventually to lead toward humanism. He also made his presence felt at Lucca, with the relief sculptures on the lunettes of the doors of San Martino, and he directly influenced a whole generation of artists. Among his followers was his son Giovanni, who in the pulpit of the church of Sant'Andrea at Pistoia achieved an incomparable degree of expressive drama. The sculptor was finally free to put his forms into motion, to see them live and breathe. The second pupil of and successor to Nicola Pisano, Arnolfo di Cambio, developed a different form of classicism that tended toward a virtually timeless staticity. In 1295 Arnolfo assumed the duties of civil and military architect of the city of Florence and designed a number of monuments that represented the origins of important stylistic developments: Santa Croce, Santa Maria del Fiore and the Palazzo della Signoria (Palazzo Vecchio). For many centuries the latter was to represent the archetypal Florentine palazzo, while the horizontality and breadth of Santa Maria del Fiore were to form the basic structure around which the genius of Brunelleschi operated.

112-113 The 13th-century church of Santa Croce is attributed to Arnolfo di Cambio.

113 left The design of the Palazzo Vecchio in Florence is attributed to Arnolfo di Cambio, who began work in 1299, incorporating the ancient tower of the Foraboschi into the building. On the right can be seen the Loggia dei Lanzi, a fine example of Florentine Gothic architecture.

113 top right The chancel, illuminated by stained-glass windows designed by Agnolo Gaddi, houses a large crucifix by a follower of Giotto and, on the walls, frescoes by Gaddi representing the Legend of the True Cross.

113 center right In the upper part of the immense Salone dei Cinquecento the grand duke of Tuscany held audiences, surrounded by Vasari's frescoes celebrating the history of Florence.

113 bottom right The first courtyard of the Palazzo Vecchio features a wealth of decoration: the fountain, the sculptures and the plants transform the space into a kind of winter garden.

The penetration of styles arriving from France was also responsible for a renewal of architectural languages. Monastic buildings, such as San Galgano or the abbey of Sant'Antimo, are examples of this mutation. In spite of the absence of its roof—which perhaps to our eyes makes it all the more suggestive—the abbey of San Galgano marks the union of Gothic "verticalism" with a Romanesque rationalism. The medley of styles is even more evident in the Duomo of Siena. This building represents a kind of summation of Sienese art, achieved through the combined work of architects, painters and sculptors from different backgrounds. The classicism of Nicola Pisano, triumphant in the pulpit, the Gothic of Giovanni Pisano, the decorations of the floor and the two-tone interior theme all contribute to a composition with few rivals. In the church of Santa Maria Novella in Florence there is evidence of a trend that could be defined as humanist. This solemn breadth, based on a human rather than divine scale, can also be seen in civil buildings such as the public palazzi of Siena and Volterra and the Bargello in Florence. At Siena, on the Piazza del Campo, the ancient *Campus Fori*, rose the palazzo designed to celebrate the splendors of local government, while on all sides rose the noble residences of the Piccolomini, the Sansedoni and the Alessi families, all built to precise, codified rules dedicated to the greater glory of the municipality. At Lucca civil building was to develop above all under the dominion of the good Paolo Guinigi, with the Villa Guinigi constructed

114-115 The Duomo of Siena is the product of the talent of innumerable artists who starting in the first half of the 13th century applied themselves to the glory of the Virgin to whom the building is dedicated. This illustration clearly shows the two-tone marble motif found throughout.

115 top Another view of the Duomo. The roof in the foreground hides the walls of the extension of the church that was never completed.

115 bottom The interior of the Duomo is extremely richly decorated, in an almost Oriental style, emphasized by the marble dressings, carvings and the decoration of the ceiling vaults.

116 top Set like a precious jewel in a valley close to Montalcino is the abbey of Sant'Antimo founded, according to popular legend, by Charlemagne. Today it is only inhabited by a small group of French monks, but each Sunday the church is filled with the faithful, attracted by the tranquility of the site and the Gregorian chants.

116 bottom The upper part of the marble facade of Santa Maria Novella in Florence was designed by Leon Battista Alberti (as was the portal), and harmonizes extraordinarily well with the lower section that is still clearly Gothic in style with Romanesque overtones.

117 top The crucifix by Coppo di Marcovaldo, carved together with his son Salerno in 1275, is to be found in the Duomo of Pistoia. Coppo di Marcovaldo has been recognized as the master of Cimabue: the suffering Christ is surrounded by scenes from the Passion.

117 bottom San Galgano, now reduced to evocative ruins, was founded by a noble knight who chose the Sienese hills in which to spend his last years as a hermit. Its decline began in the 15th century and less than a hundred years later the disaster was complete.

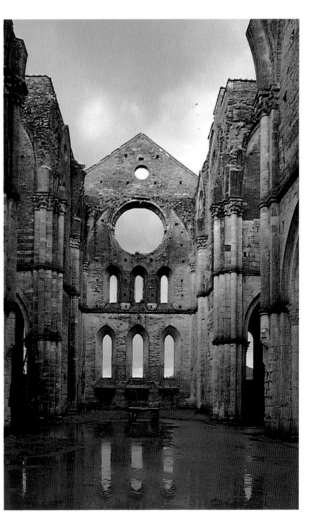

118 The frescoes
narrating the Stories
of Santa Fina in the
Collegiata at San
Gimignano were
executed by Domenico

Ghirlandaio and are
to be found in the
Renaissance setting
of the chapel by
Giuliano and
Benedetto da Maiano.

for the nobleman's out-of-town leisure and numerous palazzi built within the city walls. In the meantime the foundations were also being laid for a "revolution" in painting with a breakaway from the Byzantine stylistic motifs; Giorgio Vasari summed up this evolution when speaking of Giotto: "The art of painting changed from Greek to Latin." Others had attempted this route prior to Giotto, including Guglielmo whose crucifix in the Duomo at Sarzana depicts a Christ charged with passion and tension. Other works, such as those of Berlinghiero, Coppo di Marcovaldo and Guido di Siena, bear witness to the fervor with which art began to differentiate itself in terms of schools, influences and even political leanings. At Lucca, Romanesque painting is represented by the Berlinghiero family: the crucifix to be found in the gallery at Villa Guinigi is the only authenticated work of the father and shows, alongside certain Byzantine traces, a depth of expression that was already recognizably western. At Pistoia, Coppo di Marcovaldo—who many art historians recognize as the master of Cimabue—left a grandiose crucifix conserved in the Duomo. At Florence, it was to be Cimabue who determined the direction painting was to take, while at Siena the leading figure was Duccio di Buoninsegna. This also resulted in the dualism between Florence and Siena that was to dominate Tuscan art of the 14th century. In

119 On the right-hand side of the nave of the Collegiata (in the photo below, the interior of the church) there is a cycle of frescoes by Barna da Siena illustrating New Testament themes. From the founding of the church in the 13th century many artists contributed to its decoration: Taddeo di Bartolo, Benozzo Gozzoli, Bartolo di Fredi, as well as Domenico Ghirlandaio.

120 The two Sienese Maestà, *the one by Simone Martini (top) in the Palazzo Pubblico, and that by Duccio di Buoninsegna (bottom), now in the Museo dell'Opera Metropolitana, were painted within a few years of each other but show significant differences. Similar in compositional structure, identical in terms of subject matter, one is an affirmation of certainty, the other of doubt. One is still in the Byzantine tradition, the other displays Gothic trends.*

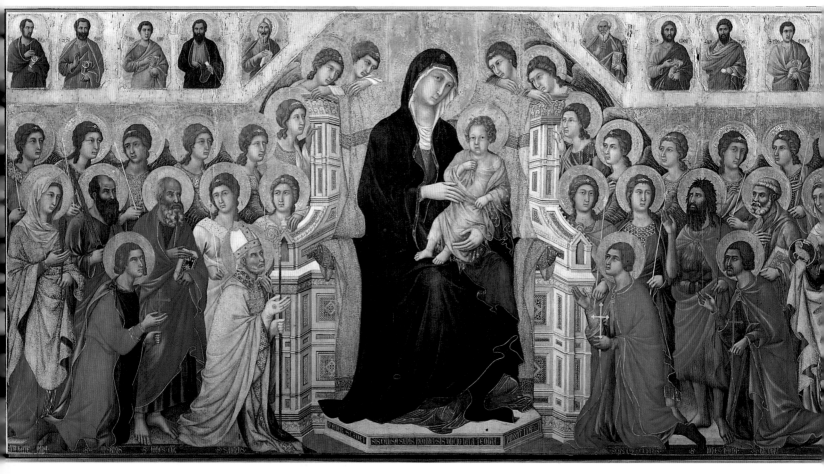

1308 the building committee of the Duomo of Siena commissioned Duccio di Buoninsegna to produce a great double-sided altar piece, the *Maestà della Madonna*. This was the work that marked Siena's definitive artistic break with Florence. As Giulio Carlo Argan was to write, "The result of the final consummation of Byzantine figuratism was, for Cimabue, a plastic condensation of the image and for Duccio a rigorously colorist anti-plastic condensation: beginning with these two, the history of painting was, in fact, to be the history of the relationship between form and color, between a plastic vision and a coloristic vision." Duccio's was a sophisticated, lyrical colorism, but one perhaps too cerebral to attract a significant following. The art of Siena was the result of a composite, open and evolved society, wealthy and proud of being so. The industriousness of the Sienese citizens was celebrated in the frescoes of the Sala della Pace in the Palazzo Pubblico: in his *Good Government* cycle Ambrogio Lorenzetti represented a life in which duty and pleasure were integrated, while in the Sala del Mappamondo Simone Martini celebrated the heraldic heroism of Guidoriccio da Fogliano riding his charger from town to town. He also tried to emulate the magic of Duccio's *Maestà*, creating an ideal of grace and vibrant beauty, of an almost courtly taste, and with a spatiality that had yet to be defined. The magnificent rise of Sienese painting was, however, destined to be short-lived, as with the death of its great masters that aristocratic sophistication was replaced with

art of a more concrete kind. Giotto was the undisputed protagonist of painting in the 14th century, a century also marked by the flourishing of so-called "vulgar" or vernacular literature. The artists and writers of the time were well aware of their Latin roots and rather than deny them they preferred to revive their ancient splendors, adding a new and fundamental element, that of nature. The intellectual aspect of Giotto's work—and this is in sharp contrast with the legend of the poor shepherd unaware of his own talent—led him to take an interest in other art forms such as architecture. He led a large workshop in Florence in which he worked with the pupils and disciples with whom he completed the frescoes of the Peruzzi and Bardi chapels in the church of Santa Croce. Toward the end of his career Giotto was appointed to the post of supervisor of building at the Duomo in Florence and in 1334 he began work on the Campanile of Santa Maria del Fiore: a three-dimensional interpretation of that clarity and purity that characterized his painting. Unfortunately, Giotto only survived to see the lower section of the tower completed. The work was eventually finished by Andrea Pisano and Francesco Talenti but without the crown planned by the maestro. Nevertheless, in spite of the alterations, the campanile is an important symbol, one of harmony and proportion, of the universality of art, the cardinal principle of the Renaissance. The classical ascendants that determined the evolution of Tuscan art also accompanied it through the late Gothic period. In Florence the renovation took place in a

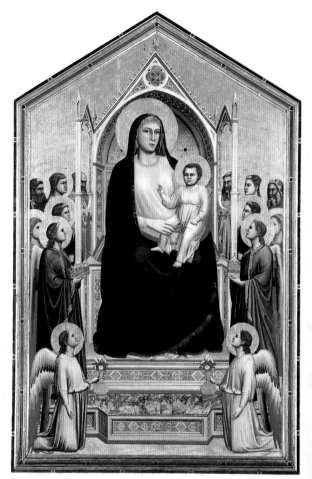

121 The Madonna *of Ognissanti, now to be found in the Uffizi, fully illustrates the power of Giotto's art, with his revolutionary sense of space, color and composition. The intense humanity of the Virgin and Child dominates, with the slim structure of the throne of secondary importance.*

well-defined political and social moment. An antithesis to the highly aesthetic, courtly taste, it favored a more concrete and, it might be said, bourgeois vision of existence. Still linked to the late Gothic, Lorenzo Ghiberti represents an expression of the transitory moment, and in the celebrated competition for the reliefs for the second pair of doors for the baptistery in Florence, he defeated in 1401 his direct rival Filippo Brunelleschi with an almost perfect composition in which pathos was, however, virtually absent. In Siena it was Jacopo della Quercia who closed the cycle. Here he left, among other works, the *Fonte Gaia*, an exaltation in candid marbles. The tomb of Ilaria del Carretto in the cathedral of San Martino at Lucca is bathed in the mystery of pure harmony. Jacopo created a sarcophagus with classical traces inserted in a composition already showing Renaissance trends, a memorial to beauty and the love of Paolo Guinigi for his tragically young wife. There are notable sculptures in almost all the churches in the countryside around Lucca: wooden Annunciations of great expressive strength such as those of Partigliano, the *Angel* by Capannori and the *San Bernardino* in Borgo a Mozzano that some critics have linked with the name of Donatello. This was the moment of three great figures who, in different fields, opened Tuscan art to the universe. Brunelleschi in architecture, Masaccio in painting and Donatello in sculpture, set out in new and original

124 Santa Maria del Fiore, the Baptistery and Giotto's Tower, in Florence form one of the world's most famous architectural compositions; a scenario that summarizes in a relatively compact area much of the history of Western art. Arnolfo di Cambio, Brunelleschi, Giotto and Ghiberti are but a few of the great artists who contributed to the decoration of the buildings.

directions that Leon Battista Alberti, scholar and architect, was to describe in his treatises dedicated to the three arts. Their new philosophy derived from the different terms in which the conception and realization of the work of art were established: where previously the contents and even the iconographical lexicon were pre-defined and certain, the artist now had to find and define them autonomously. "Art is a process of understanding, the aim of which is not so much an understanding of the object as an understanding of the human intellect, of the faculty of understanding," (Giulio Carlo Argan). This way an all-encompassing revolution that swept away all that had gone before and arose in contrast with late Gothic aestheticism. Brunelleschi mutated the very concept of space, changing it into an expression of collective secular or religious sentiments. This was a crucial moment in the secularization of an art that continued to measure itself against the divine, but also, and above all, the human, against its history and its future. The cupola of Santa Maria del Fiore in Florence, erected without scaffolding, amazed contemporaries for its audacity and technical perfection, but above all for the totally new conception of space that it preached. The Spedale degli Innocenti was also born out of an interest in town planning, and works such as the church of San Lorenzo, and the Pazzi chapel, Santo Spirito, display a fascination with the plastic potential of forms, planes and arches. Similar sentiments fueled the work of Masaccio: the space that he constructed, austere and solemn, yet intensely human and geo-

metric, was real and concrete. The miracles, the Bible and stories and the evangelical events that he depicted were all subordinated to the concept of man, the narrative being rooted in history, with no concession being made to poetics. The frescoes in the Brancacci Chapel in the Church of the Carmine, the *Trinity* in Santa Maria Novella ("We may well imagine the surprise of the Florentines when, with the veil removed, this picture was revealed that appeared to have punched a hole through the wall to show a new chapel on the other side, built according to the modern style of Brunelleschi," Gombrich), the *Madonna* and the *Santa Anna* in the Uffizi have the strength of true, ancient and modern forms with no half measures. Donatello introduced another fundamental element to art: freed of its enslavement to architecture, sculpture became a harmonious blending of lines and planes, with a degree of popular and dramatic sentiment. His wooden crucifix (in Santa Croce), accused by Brunelleschi of being a "peasant," is the exemplification of an extreme realism that fears not the slightest hint of physical unpleasantness. Donatello portrayed the men of his time, from the *David* in the Bargello to the characters in the reliefs on the baptistery font at Siena, with almost violent gestures, a far cry from the prettified and static narration of Gothic art. The three artist-symbols were, of course, not the only figures to feel that something was changing in the field of art. Following on from the genius of Ghiberti and Donatello, it would be stretching a point to define Luca della Robbia

125 Dedicated to San Giovanni Battista, the patron saint of Florence, the Baptistery, mentioned by Dante, is a splendid example of Romanesque architecture. It is finished in green-and-white marble. The interior is illuminated by the mullioned windows as well as the lantern. The cupola itself is decorated with mosaics designed by Jacopo Francescano and executed by Venetian and Florentine artists, probably including Cimabue. The dominant figure is that of Christ presiding over the final judgment.

126 *The* David *by Donatello that can be admired in the Bargello in Florence. Donatello combined the classical ideals of beauty and harmony with an understanding of a new and modern civilization.*

as an innovator, but he does deserve a place in the history of art for his invention of vitrified terra-cotta, a decorative medium that immediately obtained great success and was to become a typical product of the Florentine craftsmen, with which he executed works that combined decorative, devotional and plastic qualities, such as the choir in Santa Maria del Fiore. Giovanni da Fiesole, also known as Fra Angelico, apparently more interested in the manifestation of the divine than the new man, captured the extraordinary power of Masaccio's spatial structure. His religious vocation did not lead him to reject perspective framework, but rather he incorporated it, as can be seen in the frescoes at the San Marco convent in Florence. The great Florentine artistic movements filtered through slowly to Siena as if smothered by an obstinate traditionalism: for Sassetta and Giovanni di Paolo art was not concerned with problems of understanding or morals. Another interpreter of Masaccio's themes was Filippo Lippi, a Carmine monk and therefore in close contact with the work of the master. Paolo Uccello, with the Creation scenes in the Chiostro of Santa Maria Novella in Florence, and above all the fresco memorial to Giovanni Acuto (Sir John Hawkwood) in Santa Maria del Fiore, tackled art from yet another point of view, that of absolute rigor in which passion was excluded in the name of coherent perspective. The few surviving works by Domenico Veneziano led to a synthesis of the defined space of Brunelleschi and Masaccio with the introduction of complex structures dominated by human figures. His work ran parallel to that of Andrea del Castagno who, with the *Last Supper* at Santa Apollonia in Florence, placed the accent on an exal-

tation of the physical. However, the perfect synthesis of form, color and perspective was to be found in the work of Piero della Francesca with his solemn, timeless forms. A stranger to Florentine culture, in the works surviving at Arezzo and Borgo San Sepolcro, Piero demonstrates that he was the true pivot between Tuscan art and that of Europe. The *Legend of the True Cross* cycle in the church of San Francesco (Arezzo) represents the artist at the height of his powers when he had already completed work in Urbino, Ferrara, Rimini and his hometown of San Sepolcro: the legend loses its medieval connotations, goes beyond the storytelling role and takes on a fully Renaissance and concrete vision of the world. As Longhi wrote, "The world of Piero unfurls as bright as a colored banner wrapping itself in a calm, indifferent destiny."

We have rather neglected architecture, which after Brunelleschi—and after Leon Battista Alberti, who by the mid-15th century had traced an early synthesis of the Renaissance philosophy, placing the accent on the enthusiastic study of antiquity and noble proportions—explored forms that were perhaps less rigorous, but certainly more varied. The Villa Medicea at Poggio a Caiano that Giuliano da Sangallo designed for Lorenzo dei Medici united the simple "rusticity" of a house destined for leisure pursuits with the subtle sophistication of a classical tympanum. A fundamental name is that of Bernardo Rossellino, the only architect who succeeded in realizing, albeit only in part, the Utopian dream of an ideal city. Commissioned by Pope Pius Piccolomini II, the "Humanist Pope," Rossellini designed and reconstructed the center of the village of Corsignano in the Sienese countryside.

128-129 The Birth of Venus *by Sandro Botticelli. "The beauty that the painter wanted to exalt is a spiritual not physical beauty: the nudity of Venus signifies simplicity, purity and the absence of ornament; nature is expressed in its fundamental elements (air, water, earth); the sea rippled by the breeze blown by Aeolus and Boreas is a green-blue surface in which the waves are arranged in identical signs; the shell is also symbolic." Giulio Carlo Argan, Storia dell'Arte Italiana*

The resulting town was renamed Pienza. It featured a nucleus of coordinated buildings that were proportioned according to the demands of perspective and the town became a unique, perfect monument to the reason of mathematics and classicism. The second half of the 15th century was marked by the work of another two great masters, Antonio Pollaiolo and Sandro Botticelli. Research is the common thread between the two, although they obtained differing and frequently contrasting results. A painter and goldsmith taken under the wing of Lorenzo il Magnifico, Pollaiolo combined the sharpness of Donatello and the richness of Domenico Veneziano and was the earliest influence on Botticelli. It was the latter who was to take art from one century into the next, passing from allegorical works charged with neo-Platonism, such as *Primavera* and *The Birth of Venus*, to the last series of compositions which were loaded with tragedy, an archaic sense of religion and spirituality. We have now reached the 16th century, the era of Michelangelo, Raphael and Leonardo, but Botticelli preferred to turn back, refuting science, perspective and anatomy. Leonardo the painter began his career in the workshop of Verrocchio. His distant landscapes that form the backdrop to many works demonstrate his interest in nature and the relationship with humanity that was developed in his scientific work. A fundamental work in this sense is the unfinished *Annunciation* to be found in the Uffizi. It was Leonardo, in his few works, who brought the 15th century to a definitive close. He traveled far afield, to Milan and into France, and another of the greats, Michelangelo, was also to enjoy greater success in Rome, away from his homeland. An overview of art in the middle of the century was provided by Giorgio Vasari in his *Lives of the Artists*. He placed Michelangelo at the top of the pyramid, with those artists who, not being able to match him, preferred tiredly to imitate him, placed on the lower tiers. The young Michelangelo also enjoyed the patronage of Lorenzo, who introduced him into the neo-Platonist circle. His Florentine works, from the *David* to

129 A portrait of a lady by Antonio Pollaiolo conserved in the Uffizi galleries. A painter and sculptor, Pollaiolo started out as a goldsmith and all his works reveal a search for formal perfection, but also an interest in anatomy and limpid, luminous coloring.

130 Michelangelo's David is currently to be found in the Galleria dell'Accademia, but a faithful copy continues to stand in Piazza della Signoria, alongside the entrance to the Palazzo Vecchio. Transformed into plaster or plastic fake marble, it is also available in miniature form to tourists at all the city's souvenir stalls.

the *Tondo Doni,* from the sacristy at San Lorenzo with the tombs of Lorenzo and Giuliano dei Medici to the Laurenziana Library, display a tortuous development with profound research into nature and the spirit. The departure of Leonardo, Raphael and Michelangelo from Florence in the first decade of the 16th century left a significant vacuum. Florence itself was beginning to show signs of decline and the art world reflected this as it began a slow elaboration of the themes established by the great masters. There was no lack of important names including Frà Bartolomeo and, above all, Andrea del Sarto, who after having worked in Rome made good use of the experience in Florence, especially in the grisailles in the cloister of the Annunziata. Pontormo, on the other hand, was a more obscure figure in Tuscan Mannerism, perhaps influenced by the works of Dürer that at that time had begun to circulate in Florence. Under the patronage of the Medici, he completed a series of mythological frescoes in the villa at Poggio a Caiano in which his taste for classical culture was combined with a taut, nervous line. Tuscan architecture, in the meantime, was going through another period of great splendor with Antonio da Sangallo the Elder, the brother of Giuliano—responsible for the church of San Biagio at Montepulciano—and his nephew Antonio da Sangallo the

Younger who worked, above all, in Rome. Giorgio Vasari designed the Uffizi building, inserted between the Palazzo Vecchio, the Loggia della Signoria and the banks of the Arno, and along with Bartolomeo Ammannati was the greatest of the Mannerist architects. Ammannati was commissioned to extend Brunelleschi's Palazzo Pitti and also to build the Santa Trinita Bridge, a masterpiece of functionalism and technology. Bernardo Buontalenti, on the other hand, was invested with the honor of drawing up a town plan for Livorno. The small medieval town was cast aside in favor of an "ideal" city with wide, straight roads, geometrical piazzas and a broader more open appearance. At Pisa, a number of town-planning projects (for example Piazza dei Cavalieri) restored a dignity to the city that had since the early 15th century been somewhat overshadowed artistically speaking. In the field of sculpture, Benvenuto Cellini closed a cycle with the exaltation of technique (incomparable the pages of his celebrated autobiography in which he relates the story of the casting of the *Perseus* of the Loggia dei Lanzi at Florence commissioned by Cosimo I). This was the end of the Renaissance: along with the Grand Duchy of Ferdinand I, in the early years of the 17th century came forms of rationalism of a distinctly modern tone. Florence, in spite of its decline, still produced flashes of genius such as the

decorations of the Palazzo Pitti by Pietro da Cortona, but it was substantially cut out of the Baroque movement. In Livorno in the middle of the 19th century Leopold II worked on further extensions of the city beyond the Medici walls, with colossal projects that transformed the port, and built one of Italy's first railway stations, but these were town-planning projects designed to modernize the city. There was a long period of artistic provincialism that lasted until the mid-19th century when Florence saw the rise of the Macchiaioli movement with its post-Romantic interest in the more banal and less heroic aspects of daily life. Fattori, Signorini, Lega and Abbiati, with their domestic and military scenes, their landscapes and sketches, were among the last exponents of the Tuscan painting tradition. After them were a number of adherents to the Futurist movement.

In conclusion, a few words about one of the most significant architects of the 20th century, Giovanni Michelucci, the designer of the Santa Maria Novella railway station in Florence and the church of the Autostrada del Sole, examples of extreme compositional freedom that is at once both measured and in absolute harmony with its surroundings.

131 top left The Tondo Doni, *an early work by Michelangelo, in the Uffizi, has recently been restored after being damaged in the bloody terrorist attack that destroyed the Accademia dei Georgofili bordering the gallery.*

131 top right The Museo dell'Opera del Duomo *contains an unfinished* Pietà *by Michelangelo. The work depicts Christ in the arms of Joseph of Arithmea: it would appear that the latter figure is actually a self-portrait of the artist.*

131 bottom Begun by Giorgio Vasari on the orders of Cosimo I and continued by Buontalenti and Alfonso Parigi, the Palazzo degli Uffizi was, as the name suggests, designed to house the offices of the Florentine administrative and judicial authorities. Today it contains the State Archive and, above all, one of the world's most famous art collections, initiated by the Medici, extended by the House of Lorraine and eventually taken over by the Italian state.

136 The tall facade of San Michele in Foro, the Duomo of Lucca, is triumphantly capped with two final loggias formed from twisted columns and marble relief sculpture. The composition is *crowned by the great statue of the Archangel Michael to whom the cathedral is dedicated.*

131

INDEX

MUSEUMS AND ART COLLECTIONS

how children succeed in getting to the wrong answer. Child reasoning in his view was not simply a less accurate version of the adult variety, it was qualitatively different.

In this way, the postmodern challenge in health care research is to take some of the implications of this sort of approach a bit further. We might also see echoes of the 'strong programme's' symmetry thesis in the social study of science. Whether beliefs are true or false is a matter for the seekers after knowledge themselves. To the researcher they are all equally interesting. To the postmodernist researcher, moreover, every aspect of what can be seen, heard, touched or smelt in a health care setting is important. The ceremonies of giving and receiving care, the 'liturgy of the clinic', is just as important as the members' pharmacological theories about what the medications do.

Postmodernism has foregrounded the way that knowledge may be intimately related to power structures and that mainstream knowledge marginalizes the viewpoints of disempowered social groups. In the variants of postmodern thinking that take their cue from Michel Foucault, knowledge is seen in terms of historical processes and the exercise of power. The development of psychiatry as a medical speciality has not happened because maladies of the mind are somehow naturally part of the purview of medicine, in this view. It has happened as a result of a long process of historical struggle as doctors sought to expand their territory. The same could be said for the medicalization of sex. It is not naturally or inherently medical but a series of historical, political and scientific manoeuvres over the past 300 or 400 years have made it so. Much postmodernist thinking, then, has drawn upon – but is not coterminous with – earlier critiques of heath care provision from feminist, Marxist and anti-racist scholars, yet in its attempt to be inclusive, some would argue it has lost the political edge of these earlier positions and fails in its account of material inequality. The regress into phenomenologically based considerations of people's thinking, experience and local social orders has made it difficult to think clearly about oppression and inequality. However, postmodernism also opens up the possibility of thinking about the operation of power in new ways. Let us try to illustrate what we mean. One way of thinking about this is by analogy with gardening. Put crudely, the conceptions of power in much historical materialist critical thinking sees the exercise of power as being a bit like weed-killer. It oppresses, distorts, denies our potential and reduces us as human beings. Within postmodern conceptions of power, it is much more like topiary, in that it encourages social institutions and people to grow in particular ways. In this vein, maybe, as Parker *et al.* (1995) note, the crucial feature of health care systems is not whether they 'cure' people, but whether they are successful in attaching pathological identities to vulnerable people. Thus developing an identity as a 'schizophrenic' or 'substance abuser' may not result in a 'cure' – quite the contrary – but it provides an identity for the person so named and an explanation as to why the attempted interventions fail. As Rose (1990) has documented, the flourishing of psychology and psychiatry over the past century and a half have given us new ways to think about ourselves and one another.

Another way of thinking about knowledge from a postmodern perspective that we have found useful with students is to think of it like railways. The rise of science, like the contemporaneous rise of rail transport, allowed the exploration and exploitation of new territories and resources. Both railways and science have facilitated universal

standards of business, timekeeping and social practice. Yet both also transform the territory they are built through, allowing new patterns of exploitation, living arrangements and human geographies. Postmodernism provides some clues as to how we might think about the relationship between knowledge and the societies which produce it and within which it has meaning.

From our point of view, the postmodernist movement, if it can be called such, has implications for how we think about research in health care. That is, it calls into question the assumption that science is progressive and that knowledge flourishes with the growth of research. It also foregrounds the possibility that research which works and produces clinically useful knowledge in one place will not do so in others. The most far-reaching implication of postmodernism for the philosophy of science and the conduct of enquiry is its radical anti-foundationalism. That is, reality is not something which is 'out there' in any simple sense. In terms of its implications for research, consider, for example, ethnomethodology and conversation analysis. These approaches invite us to consider whether and how people build physical and social realities in their conversations and social interaction patterns. They are concerned with the method that ordinary people ('ethnos') use to navigate their way through social life. In other words, like postmodernism, these approaches adhere to an anti-foundationalist approach and take seriously the strategies people use to convince others of the truth of their 'reality'. As Schegloff (1997) urges, the Archimedian point of leverage should be sought in the interaction itself. In deciding what is relevant or what is happening, the analyst should, in Schegloff's view, look at the people to whom it matters most – the interactants themselves. If you think you see inequalities at work in a setting, look to see whether the participants themselves are talking about inequalities or showing clear signs of dominance or deference. From this point of view, if one were to look at people in health settings, one might wish to consider how interactants work together to construct notions of health, illness and disability and apply them to the particular case in question. For example, in the previous chapter, Maynard's (1991) studies of the process of giving and receiving diagnostic news have shown how the reality of a patient's problems results from a complex dance whereby the patient's, professionals' and relatives' views are brought into alignment. Thus, practitioners and clients are very much practical philosophers as they go about their health care tasks of being ill and providing treatment. This offers the possibility that different interactional dances could yield very different accounts of clients and their problems and is a potentially challenging and destabilizing perspective within health care. Rather than just being an academic exercise, it might be possible for this approach to be used to help practitioners imagine how their own realities are constrained by the terminology they use and the interactions they participate in.

One implication of taking postmodern ideas seriously in health care research is to recognize the sheer diversity of views, beliefs and practices that health care encompasses. The interactions that practitioners, clients and researchers participate in may involve very different perspectives and world-views on the part of the various members (Green and Britten 1998). Qualitative studies performed under the umbrella of postmodernism often take the interaction itself as a focus of research. This marks them as distinct from research in a more positivistic mould, which often

pre-defines what the factors under study will be. This focus on interaction highlights the diversity of viewpoints in clinical encounters. Katon and Kleinman (1981) viewed consultations between doctors and patients as the synthesis of conflicting explanatory systems about health and illness. This potential conflict required careful negotiation to achieve a satisfactory outcome. The clinical consultation may be a meeting between very different views of reality (Mishler 1984). Qualitative researchers, often working from within a postmodern – or at least a relativistic – perspective, have shown the importance of taking these competing perspectives and explanatory systems at face value. Green and Britten (1998) give the example of studies of asthma sufferers in the context of their adherence to recommended medication regimes. Although the official medical 'reality' is that asthma medication reduces morbidity and mortality, and can benefit users, qualitative studies disclose a very different 'reality' for patients themselves. First, some patients have negative views about the medications, believing them to be 'unnatural' substances that diminish the body's own ability to fight disease and cause dependency (Britten 1994). Doctors, on the other hand, make the common-sensical assumption that patients consult them because they are seeking medication (Hull and Marshall 1987). This is borne out in studies of patients with asthma by Osman *et al.* (1993), which show that patients worry about becoming physically and psychologically dependent on bronchodilators, and worry about the long-term effects of inhaling corticosteroids (Hewett 1994). Now from a medical point of view one might wish to dismiss these concerns or reassure patients. However, as Green and Britten (1998) note, regarding patients' realities as ignorant or misguided and attempting to persuade them of the value of a biomedical approach have limited value in increasing adherence. Green and Britten urge the need to recognize and incorporate patients' perspectives to ensure a better treatment outcome experience. One might even go further and ask how it is that patients and professionals decide whether a particular outcome is desirable, or whether an experience is an outcome or merely coincidental. In a sense, the very terms themselves are up for grabs.

Within philosophy itself, the interest in postmodernism goes back a little earlier than its sudden arrival in the health care disciplines. Some of the first flurry of interest can be traced to the publication in English of the works of Jaques Derrida (e.g. 1977). He pursued the fascination with language even further. His contention was that words, sentences and language itself have no fixed meaning and the relationship between language and the world is indeterminate. The slogan 'there is nothing outside the text' is attributed to him. He has also pointed to the internal contradictions in texts themselves, and the inadequacy of what he calls 'logocentrism', the idea that words express things in the mind, or describe things in nature. His view that language cannot express ideas and concepts in the mind is closely bound up with his critique of phenomenology, inasmuch as language cannot express consciousness in any simple sense. This suggestion that language is somehow all we have is also found in the work of the psychoanalyst Jaques Lacan (1977), who contended that our psychic contents, especially our unconscious, are structured in and through language. In particular, it is not a language which transparently reflects either reality or our thoughts, for it is subject to a whole variety of processes of condensation and displacement as theorized by Freud, as well as being highly metaphoric and metonymic and imbued with patriarchal ideology. In a sense, then, consciousness,

and indeed the self, are kinds of allegorical stories. Or possibly they are multiple, allegorical stories.

The possibility that there are multiple stories about nature, rather than a single reliable epistemology, has, as we have seen, been a central plank in postmodern theory. For example, Lyotard (1984) has contended that the twentieth century saw the collapse of what he calls 'grand narratives', the hopeful stories that we are making progress, proceeding towards enlightenment, or towards the betterment of the human condition. This was the story behind positivism, but also Marxism, psychoanalysis and most of the nineteenth-century schemes for the improvement of our circumstances. Instead, Lyotard argues that we have a multiplicity of competing language-games and it is impossible to judge any one of these in terms of any other. It is therefore not possible, in this view, to perform critique, to enlighten or to achieve rational consensus. This story is reminiscent of the Tower of Babel, such that the grand projects to improve the lot of humanity have disintegrated into competing interest groups spouting incommensurable languages.

Postmodernism, then, represents a far-reaching paradigm shift in which 'reality has been replaced with simulation, rationality by multivocality, monolithic organization by fragmentation, and grand theories by plans' (Spitzer 1998, p. 164). Postmodernism is associated with a scepticism bordering on incredulity towards the so-called grand narratives and an abandonment of the search for a stable reality on which to anchor our claims to knowledge. Instead, in this view, the world is constituted by 'differance' (Derrida 1978; Lyotard 1984; Sarup 1988; Boyne 1992; Fox 1993; Gurevitz 1997; Spitzer 1998).

The suggestion that knowledge is a form of power and that regimes of truth are made to work through a range of coercive practices has also been rediscovered, from Bacon and Nietzsche, and has been expressed most strongly in the work of Michel Foucault (e.g. 1965). Foucault was interested in how knowledge itself was not a neutral servant of humanity but tended to constitute the 'subject' – the individual – in particular ways. The 'knowledge' of nymphomania and masturbatory insanity helps to constitute the individuals who allegedly suffer from what we now admit to be highly questionable, if not humorous maladies. One could perhaps say the same in our own time about the knowledge of 'sex addiction' or 'co-dependency'. The idea that we have access only to representations, through language or imagery, and never the 'real thing' is elaborated in some detail by Baudrillard (1990). He would appreciate the irony that the term 'real thing' has been hijacked as a Coca-Cola advertising slogan. He argued that the 1991 Gulf War 'never happened' because it took place largely on television (Baudrillard 1995). All we have access to is endless simulation, a hyperreal world where simulations become more lifelike and vibrant than the lacklustre realities they have left behind. Father Christmas was usually depicted in grey clothing until 1931 when he appeared in a red and white outfit as part of a winter advertising campaign run by Coca-Cola. The advertising-enhanced version soon outstripped the older incarnation. The hyperreal supervenes over the real. In health, the currently fashionable drive to 'detox' the body has very little to do with sober scientific research on the optimum concentration of certain chemicals in the tissues, and there is often neither funding nor personnel to conduct such research anyway. The momentum of

the cultural phenomenon is to do with whether it sounds like it could be scientific. The analysis of these phenomena is more readily accomplished if we look not so much at the biochemistry or earnest scientific 'protocol statements' about nature, but grasp the hyperreal surface directly.

Language, simulation and representation have always been central to the theory and practice of a good deal of health care, much of which is transacted through language: in day-to-day verbal and written communications involving staff, patients and relatives; in counselling; in patient records and care planning. Recently, the demand for health care practitioners to communicate effectively both in speech and writing has become more urgent. Health care practice must now satisfy a wide audience of clients, purchasers, professional bodies and the law. However, while there has been a good deal of research on doctor–patient interaction, scholars have only recently begun to focus on language in nursing, occupational therapy, physiotherapy and other professions allied to medicine. Work on clinical encounters has only occasionally focused on pharmacists, audiologists, speech therapists or dentists. Because this fundamental concern has not been sufficiently emphasized, language has been used frequently by health care professionals themselves as if it were somehow a transparent means of communicating. This naivety has been revealed in a lack of awareness of the way in which words impact upon care and has left practitioners sometimes ill-equipped to deal with challenges to define exactly what they mean by the language they use.

For anyone to define what exactly they mean by the language they use is, of course, no easy matter. A huge academic industry has grown up around the question of language, trying to establish what language does, how it can achieve meaning, whether it mirrors or creates reality, to what extent human beings and their cultures are constructed by language, how powerful it is, how ideological it is. Disciplines as diverse as philosophy, linguistics and anthropology, literary criticism, psychology and sociology, have tackled the problem of language and meaning.

An increased scepticism about accepted values and a greater willingness to question what has gone before has also characterized the spirit of postmodernism, which can be seen in almost every aspect of life. Although great emphasis is placed on the importance of evidence-based heath care and reflective practice, these very notions are problematic. Ideas about what constitutes evidence and practice itself may be controversial. There is a multitude of ways in which nursing activities may be understood, described, justified or disseminated. Often, a variety of ideas will be in competition with each other and not result in any clear-cut pathways for care.

This kind of problem surrounds a general debate about the nature of meaning and language which is at the core of the whole discourse or condition of postmodernism. To recapitulate, postmodernism, like the ideas and philosophies it seeks to describe, is difficult to define. In part, it is to do with increasing scepticism of about the ability of 'grand narratives' to explain and improve the human condition. In health care, there is a growing feeling that much of what is done in the name of treatment may be ineffective, expensive and sometimes harmful. The grand narratives that accounted for human life have been eroded to the point that we are no longer sure about what it means to be human and how to live our lives. This is liberating for some while threatening to others. Postmodernism, then, broadly concerns the rootlessness

of late twentieth-century life, the fragmentation of institutions and the wild pro-liferation of the media.

In the UK, it could be argued that what has happened to the health service with its fragmentation into purchasers, providers and fund-holders and the loss of a coherent institutional framework is a prime example of a postmodernist world. More generally, we now live in a world of hyper-communication; information technology churns out vast amounts of texts and images so that stable meanings are difficult to detect. Paradox and uncertainty rule.

Within the postmodernist world-view, emphasis is placed on discourse or 'lan-guage in use' as the substance of social life. Reality becomes something that is con-structed by language. Thinkers such as Jaques Derrida have cast considerable doubt over the possibility of a resolution to the issues around meaning and language. Although postmodernism prioritizes language as a major feature of social life, its insistence that meanings are only local, provisional and controversial and that our methods of enquiry are value-laden mean that it is difficult to make any definite statements about the world.

Postmodernism itself has resisted definition: whether postmodernism represents a sharp break from modernity or simply a late stage in that historical development has been debated. In a sense, the question 'what is postmodernism?' is a profoundly modernist question. It may well not be possible to answer it from within postmodern-ism itself. Debates have focused on three overlapping terrains: the *experience* of contemporary reality (subjectivity and identity); the *representation* of the contempor-ary (in the arts, architecture, the media, advertising and consumer goods); and the *analysis* of the contemporary (the state of knowledge in postmodern society) (Scannell *et al.* 1992, p. 2). Yet even amid this uncertainty, there are some features that cut across most postmodernist claims: 'Postmodernism mistrusts all modernist claims to ground an understanding of the contemporary social world in scientific rationality' (Scannell *et al.* 1992, p. 3). The relationship between modernism and postmodernism is often central to the definition of the latter. It is almost as if postmodernism is defined by what it lacks rather than what it contains:

> Modernism acknowledged the fragmentary, transient, dislocated character of the social world but tried to overcome it, to retrieve a lost unity, whereas postmodern-ism is content to accept and celebrate a de-centred political, economic and cul-tural global environment. It rejects deep structures, any notion of an underlying, determining reality. It accepts a world of appearances, a surface reality without depth.
>
> (Scannell *et al.* 1992, p. 3)

Thus, in health care, a modernist ambition might be to try to find out what the patient's real problem is and to do this by the use of stethoscopes, blood tests, CAT scans and diagnostic interviews. The idea is that however incoherent the patient's symptoms, there must be some unitary underlying pathology that can be discovered by the skilled clinician. From a postmodernist perspective, the patient's worry about who will feed her cat is as much a feature of the illness experience as the swelling, fracture or blood test results.

Postmodernism lends its weight, then, to a growing tradition of scepticism about health care. As Lewis (2000) reminds us, in the West medicine benefited from tremendous popular support in the first three-quarters of the twentieth century. But, increasingly, this support is evolving into a chorus of criticisms. Over the past quarter of a century, health care providers have been rebuked. Edmund Pellegrino, writing nearly a quarter of a century ago, criticized health care specialists for a long list of shortcomings, including: overspecialization; technicism; overprofessionalism; insensitivity to personal and sociocultural values; too narrow a construal of the doctor's role; too much 'curing' rather than 'caring'; not enough emphasis on prevention, patient participation and patient education; too much economic incentive; a 'trade school' mentality; overmedicalization of everyday life; inhumane treatment of medical students; overwork by house staff; and deficiencies in verbal and non-verbal communication (Pellegrino 1979). To this list identified by Pellegrino, Lewis (2000) adds the current debates and disaffections around the issues in health economics where critics have pointed to increasing costs yet profound inequalities in access.

In Lewis's view, the situation is even more acute in mental health care. In the USA, and to some extent in the UK, psychiatry suffers from all of these problems and more. Psychiatry is the only specialty which has a protest movement ('antipsychiatry', 'mad pride' and so on) organized against it. People who might once have been treated in clinics are now increasingly found struggling in prisons, shelters or in the streets. As Lewis puts it, 'Psychiatrists are having more and more of their procedures denied, psychiatric hospitals are closing, research money is dwindling (except for the problematic funds coming from pharmaceuticals), and fewer and fewer residents are pursuing psychiatry as a career choice' (Lewis 2000, p. 72). Yet, in spite of its clearly beleaguered status, psychiatry continues to organize its core knowledge structures with few significant changes aside from a drift towards an even greater reliance on neuroscience, biochemistry and genetics as sources of explanation for the disorders it tries to deal with.

If we take postmodernist thinking at face value, there are disturbing implications for the practice of health care (Clarke 1996). If it is impossible for researchers and practitioners to reach a satisfactory understanding of what they do, if reality is indeed indeterminate, how do they know that they're doing any good? How can researchers be sure that the data they have so painstakingly gathered will not become hopelessly outdated in a short time? There is, nonetheless, something to be salvaged from the postmodernist assault on convention. It can sensitize us to the fact that there may be conflicting opinions about illness, unexplored dimensions and different layers of reality. What doctors know is different from what nurses know and differs again from the patient's experience. Postmodernism allows us to grasp this diverse picture without feeling the need to establish 'the truth'.

In a sense, some health care disciplines were drifting in this direction long before the term postmodernism was in common currency. Nursing began to define itself as a discipline that was primarily concerned with interpersonal and communicative issues a full half century ago with Peplau's famous book (Peplau 1952). This interpersonal dimension has been underscored in the work of other nurse scholars. Virginia Henderson consolidated nursing's role as an interpersonal process when she wrote: 'The unique function of the nurse is to assist the individual, sick or well, in the

performance of those activities contributing to health, or its recovery (or to a peaceful death) that he would perform unaided if he had the necessary strength or will' (Henderson 1966, p. 15).

Here, the modernist project, with its technically skilled individuals focusing their powers on the individual is clearly visible. Yet at the same time, the emphasis on interpersonal processes is also beginning to subvert the focus on the more archetypal modernist matters of science. This dilemma, between the modernist focus on the individual and the postmodern concern with specificity and local activities can be seen in the present day too. Dougan (1995) puts it thus: 'the philosophy of nursing in the 1990s is firmly rooted in recognising people as individuals with specific wants and needs' (p. 63). There are a number of different strands in this form of thinking. On the one hand, there are tendencies which are profoundly modernist – for example, the idea of wants and needs reinforces the Cartesian notion of the individual who is captain of his or her own ship and can thus be persuaded to take responsibility for his or her own health through social psychological techniques designed to manipulate their 'attitudes' or 'health beliefs'. On the other hand, the individuality and specificity of the process of nursing and the disarticulation of the process of nursing from enlightenment project science. As the structure of health care changes and health care delivery is reorganized, the postmodern condition may involve nurses in more holistic care for their clients and might involve a reorganization of care at a local level so as to empower clients (Lister 1997, p. 42). Indeed, nurses may be able to become even more client-focused in that spaces may be opened up for new approaches to care that have hitherto been marginalized, such as complementary therapies. On the other hand, the relative instability, constant reorganization and the break-up of nationally organized systems of care into competing organic units may force health care into a situation which emphasizes market forces at the expense of client care. The model of health care delivery appears to involve a larger number of small, organic organizations competing for trade. As Lister (1997) and Morgan (1986) note, this is curiously reminiscent of a kind of social Darwinism and an implicit endorsement of market forces. In this way, it seems to subscribe to the idea that competition is inevitable and that the capitalist system is a natural and implacable fact.

Such diversity in the forms of provision for health care and the diversity in meanings that can be assigned to language adds up to a 'strain' on the use of language. Health care practitioners need to be aware of this strain; the words they speak or write may convey meanings they did not anticipate or desire. While carers and researchers, like everyone else, can never guarantee the meanings of their spoken or written words, this diversity means that there is a vastly increased scope for misinterpretation and this requires a constant vigilance or self-surveillance when considering the meanings of one's own or other people's spoken and written texts. The strain on meaning in language, combined with the power of language to construct the world in which we live, makes it more important than ever for practitioners to monitor health care language as it affects the lives of others.

Postmodernism also tackles the style and substance of writing in the health sciences and attempts to reformulate it in a way that brings in a wider variety of issues than are conventionally included in academic writing. Here is Nicholas Fox, who

produced a good deal of writing in the early 1990s based on his experiences as a participant observer in a hospital, describing what he was trying to do in his book *The Social Meaning of Surgery*:

> I was conscious of how visual were the events that I wished to record. Along with the smell – a sense often omitted from ethnography – the visual does not necessarily translate easily into a written record, and I have often imagined the kind of visual ethnography of surgery which I should like to produce – something between 'Your Life in Their Hands' and a piece of 'new journalism'. Certainly, both kinds of media are evocative, and I share Tyler's sentiment (1986) that ethnography should have evocation as its task.
>
> (Fox 1992, p. ix)

In a similar vein, here are Lather and Smithies talking about their work on AIDS:

> This is organized as layers of various kinds of information, shifts in register, turns of different faces toward the reader, in order to provide a glimpse of the vast and intricate network of the complexities of cultural information about AIDS in which we are all caught. Although this book is not so much planned confusion as it might at first appear, it is, at some level, about what we see as a breakdown of clear interpretation and confidence in the ability/warrant to tell such stories in uncomplicated, non-messy ways.
>
> (Lather and Smithies 1997, p. xvi)

These are both manifesto statements of researchers trying to explore the possibility of new styles of writing in health care scholarship. As Abma (2002) notes, a great many scholars in the qualitative and postmodern traditions have observed the shortcomings of conventional writing and have taken the risk of presenting their findings in non-traditional ways. A great many qualitative researchers are experimenting with hitherto unexplored forms of narrative representation for their work. For example, workers have explored literary forms that include poetry (Richardson 1993; Glesne 1997), (auto)biography (hooks 1990; Barone 1997; Denzin 1999; Ellis and Bocher 2000), *testimonio* (Beverley 2000), ethno-drama and fiction (Pfohl 1992) and theatre plays (Falk and Perron 1995). There are also examples of people promoting and exploring the use of non-literary forms, including photo essays (Lapidus 1996), video (Abma 1998), music (Kivnick 1996), theatre (Mienczakowski 1995) and dance performances (Blumenfeld-Jones 1995). As Abma (2002) notes, like Fox, these writings and performances aim to be evocative so as to draw the audience in. This perhaps will enable audience members to experience the topic from a variety of perspectives and to be 'touched at an emotional level' (Abma 2002, p. 6). The figurative styles of expression deployed by these authors can readily be distinguished from the more sober, narrowly descriptive, toneless language of conventional social science writing. Although the insistence on traditional research writing has been stronger in the health disciplines than in education and the humanities (Norris 1997, p. 90), qualitative health researchers have also been drawn to explore these new forms of representation to present their findings.

Language in action

Despite the pervading sense that meaning in language is problematical, many theorists have tried to arrive at plausible interpretations of what words can do and mean. The Speech Act Theory of Austin (1962), Searle (1969) and Grice (1975) has been useful in this regard – examining how actions are performed through speech. Recent developments in conversation analysis and discourse analysis show up some fundamental problems in medico-nursing knowledge. From a conversation-analytic perspective, speakers are not simply conversing about a world that is external to them, but are mutually constructing it. Discourse analysis draws attention to the way in which repertoires of health care language produce the sense that carers are talking about a world that is external to their patients.

In much analysis of the nature of language, there is a tendency for the written text to be considered more important than the spoken word. For example, in grammar, what we call the 'parts of speech' are usually based on the language as it is written. In health care situations, too, the fact that written records are permanent and that they are very important if legal issues arise or patients complain mean that they are often given a higher status than what has been said. The written language of health care can be analysed in reports, care plans and patients' notes and it is easy to see how verbal communications between doctors, nurses, students, social workers and other staff are informed by the linguistic structure of written records.

It is not, perhaps, immediately apparent that what practitioners say in spoken or written texts are also actions. But actions they are. When a health care professional, for example, orders a patient to stop doing something, the effect of the words may well be that the patient does indeed stop. Here the words 'Stop that!' can be seen to have a similar power to the act of physically stopping someone from doing something. Equally, the way that health professionals judge a person in written and spoken text may well act against the person in a very obvious way. Staff may communicate that a client is 'manipulative' and this negative tag then affects how that client feels about himself if it is said directly to him, or the way in which others respond to him if such a meaning is conveyed in spoken or written reports to others. Such negative communicative acts are far from the ideal of promoting well-being. Since health care staff perform a variety of speech acts in their daily work, it is clearly important to examine them critically.

Telling stories about distress – from modernism to postmodernism

Health professionals make sense of the world in which they work by drawing on the resources of meaning with which their culture and trainings provide them. This is not surprising, as the scientific story we learn about the practice of health care has a sense of coherence and optimism. Since the eighteenth century, sometimes known as the Age of Reason, the belief that the world will yield its secrets to scientific enquiry has been extremely popular in Europe and the United States (Hollinger 1994). This belief is associated with the view that rational, systematic means of acquiring knowledge are the best, and that knowledge should be based on scientifically derived facts.

The distinction between modernism and postmodernism can be seen at work here. Modernism is the perspective still taken by most textbooks of psychology, psychiatry and nursing, which carefully avoid what the authors consider to be myths, superstitions or metaphysics. Modernism is associated with what has been called an 'up the mountain' theory of science, which proclaims that we know far more now than we ever did in the past, and that practice and treatment are getting better as time goes on. The naivety and cruelty of medicine and nursing in the past are contrasted with the enlightened, humane and caring approach of the present day. The modernist point of view (e.g. Ritzer 1992) is often sustained by some grand narrative as to the nature of the material world, such as that human consciousness can ultimately be explained in terms of brain chemistry. Michel Foucault (1975) has argued that, from its inception, 'The science of man . . . was medically based' (p. 36). The education of health professionals is pervaded with such assumptions.

Allied to this outlook is the notion that individuals are the authors of their own ideas, speech or writing. From Descartes' assertion, 'I think; therefore, I am', to contemporary concern with individuals' thoughts, emotions and actions, the idea of authorship or responsibility has been essential to the sciences and humanities.

Postmodernism takes a very different stance. Postmodernists do not find the world to be ordered and coherent and consider grand narratives doomed to failure. Postmodernism is a loose collection of philosophies which emphasize difference rather than unity, fragmentation rather than integration, and the minority or unusual point of view rather than the majority or mainstream viewpoint. Postmodern thinkers are often concerned with language: 'Language is now necessarily the central consideration in all attempts to know, act and live' (Lemert 1990, p. 234). Lemert (1990) and Ritzer (1992) explain that scientific theories are texts – we usually encounter them in written form. Lyotard (1984) argues that 'Scientific knowledge is a form of discourse' (p. 3). And the empirical reality to which scientific theories apply is often textual as well. In nursing, care plans, patient records, the wider body of theory and research on which practice is based, all are texts. Almost every part of health care, certainly as it is performed by people directly involved with clients, is mediated through language. Clarke (1996) argues that a postmodernist perspective requires nurses to 'connect with the devolved needs/wants of patients, in respect of their autonomy and medication, and cease pursuing abstract, doctrinaire ideals' (p. 261).

In his book *The Precession of Simulacra*, Baudrillard suggests an underlying sense of melancholy inherent in postmodern experience that is the result of inhabiting a world of ambivalence. He writes of 'a liquidation of all referentials' (Baudrillard 1983, p. 4), the result of a proliferation of images that replace previous notions of truth with an ever-changing world of simulation (Clayton 2002). This melancholy is marked by the way we feel about the world: 'Our age is characterised by invisible latent threats working quietly in the air we breathe and the bodies we inhabit' (Mansfield 2000, pp. 169–70).

Postmodernism encourages a greater sensitivity to the local concerns of patients. For many years, nursing education was a matter of learning about hygiene and practising techniques and memorizing procedures, the grand narratives of biomedical models of health. More recently, nursing thinking has come to emphasize more strongly the caring role of nurses and the importance of nurses reflecting critically on

their practice. This might be described as the beginnings of a postmodern conscious-ness among nurses.

The importance of texts in health care has been increasingly recognized as scholars strive to understand the nursing process. As Cheek and Rudge (1994) say, 'nursing and nursing practice can be considered to represent a reality which is text-ually mediated' (p. 15). The turn to texts in nursing scholarship is also associated with a scepticism of 'grand narratives' – Darbyshire (1994) warns us off sets of abstract principles in making sense of health care practice. The postmodern concern with minority points of view has led some to ask why conventional health care research ignores the 40 million Americans without health care (Allen 1995).

Postmodernism itself contains some interesting paradoxes too. On the one hand, it is associated with a tendency to overthrow stable notions of the self, with the notion of *cogito ergo sum* instead reminding us that selves are contrived, constructed and liable to be shattered as our circumstances change. On the other hand, the question of authorship is also central in postmodern scholarship because the author of a text is seen as crucial. A scientific paper, for example, cannot, in the postmodern view, be seen as a transparent window on reality, but will instead be seen as reflecting the interests and cultural location of the researchers and authors. There are a number of pieces of contemporary scholarship that attempt to look at the professional discourses of the helping professions in this way. The entities, concepts and findings that have been so painstakingly elicited from tragic clinical experiences and through meticulous observation and research are increasingly called into question. The questioning is not necessarily aimed at the integrity or honesty of the clinicians and researchers. Rather, it is directed at the very foundation of the categories and concepts themselves.

To take an example of this, consider a contemporary category that has arguably been constructed in this way: attention deficit hyperactivity disorder. As Laurence and McCallum (1998) ask, to what extent is this category being developed to aid the management of troublesome children? Perhaps psychiatry is engaged in a attempt at 'the production and maintenance of social normality and competence' (Rose 1996). Laurence and McCallum (1998) go on to say, 'the possibility of thinking and acting on modern categories of child arose from governmental attempts to know and under-stand the disruptive individual by means of techniques of calculability which carved out a new space – the space "inside the child's head" – for the operation of power'. That is, even when we can find youngsters to appear on television to attest to the benefits the drug Ritalin has brought them, and how it has enabled them to conquer their 'illness', this does not necessarily tell us very much about the nature of the problem. It may just as easily reflect the fact that the drug companies are funding the support group to which their parents belong (Breggin 2000). It might well be through social manoeuvres that the idea of a person's healthy core becomes detached from the parts of themselves which appear to be undesirable. Concept formulations, then, might be involved in supporting the moral order, such that we can identify parts of ourselves which are alien and which must be conquered, while the failures in our social institutions can be attributed to the actions of a few bad apples with medical pathologies.

However, once we look at the conceptual diversity that exists in some fields, it is a little difficult to sustain this idea of concepts being somehow constructed with a

certain set of governmental interests in mind. Some areas of health care do have such a fragmented field of activities and concerns, with a large number of individuals with few ideas in common yet all of whom are more or less engaged in the same practices. People often don't share concepts, even though they appear to be involved in the same system of suffering and healing. For example, Lee-Treweek (2002) examines complementary medicine and considers how the clients and the professionals involved may have rather different understandings of what is going on in the therapy itself. As Lee-Treweek discovered, many of the clients attending a cranial osteopath had theories of the treatment that departed from the manifest position of the discipline itself. For example, they said things like 'is he not putting out signals and getting the blood flowing?' (Lee-Treweek 2002, p. 60). Some of the clients were even more vague about what was going on: 'I have to say I don't know the name of what he does I think it's cranial cranio something. But I think it's like acupressure which is putting your fingers in specific points to release tension . . . the main thing is to balance out your body so you're not pulling off to one side and your muscles aren't pulling you over' (Lee-Treweek 2002, pp. 62–3). That is, the clients were using and grouping concept formulations together in a way that seemed to them to be sensible, deploying analogies between the cranial osteopathy treatment and acupressure; ideas about getting blood moving around the body, fluid intake and toxins were used by clients, but not in a way that corresponded with the 'official version' of events. Cranial osteopathy, as it was originally conceived by William Garner Sutherland in the late nineteenth century, relies on the idea that there are minute movements in the plates of the skull and that any restriction of these 'breathing' movements would lead to physical, psychological and emotional problems (Sutherland Society 2001). Even more interesting, from our point of view, is that while osteopathy is often thought of as a complementary or perhaps holistic therapy, the practitioner in Lee-Treweek's study did not think of himself as performing holistic therapy, though perhaps his clients thought he was.

This example could no doubt be multiplied if we studied a number of different topic areas. The point is that there are a number of incommensurable concept formulations in the healing encounter and they do not necessarily have to come into alignment for there to be a sense of benefit to the client. Indeed, maybe it is the incommensurability of concept formulations that enables everyone to proceed as if all was well. If people actually knew about the concepts that the other members held, then the veneer of accord might be ruptured.

The veneer of accord that contemporary critical and postmodern scholars seek to rupture can be seen in some of the guiding assumptions of health care too. Whereas it has often been taken for granted that a 'positive attitude' is desirable for clients of the caring professions, there are some who sound a note of caution about this. Held (2002) notes that according to both popular and professional indicators, the push for the positive attitude in America is on the rise. She considers this popular culture *Zeitgeist* and notes that it appears in psychotherapeutic disciplines as diverse as 'positive psychology' and so-called 'postmodern therapy'. Held sees both of these as resting on a foundation of optimism and positive thinking despite their opposing views about a proper philosophy of science. She notes that cross-cultural evidence does not necessarily support the North American assumption that a positive attitude is necessary for a sense of well-being. She also notes findings in health psychology,

clinical and counselling psychology, and organizational studies that undermine the assumption that accentuating the positive and eliminating the negative is necessarily beneficial in terms of physical and mental health. Held calls this assumption the 'tyranny of the positive attitude'. Moreover, this invites the possibility that the unprecedented pressure to accentuate the positive could itself contribute to some forms of unhappiness. This possibility of entertaining paradox is also a feature of postmodernist thinking. Striving for consistency is a characteristic of modernist discourse, whereas the postmodern tendency is to observe and celebrate the 'play' within the structures.

The postmodern tendency to explore contradictions and divergences can lead us to examine hitherto under-exploited crevices and schisms in the fabric of experience. For example, there are some curious tensions in how we think about health and disease. Take the case of Caesarean sections in giving birth. In some parts of the world, the incidence of this operation is much higher than others. In Western Europe, Australia and North America, where rates are very high, there is a good deal of concern about whether the operations are strictly necessary. There is also a concern that this represents a kind of medicalization of childbirth on the part of the health care professions and that control is being taken away from women themselves. Studies such as that by Fenwick *et al.* (2003) disclose unpleasant feelings on the part of women who have had a Caesarean, such as those who feel that the fact they have had a Caesarean means that they are inadequate or that the experience of birth has been taken away from them.

On the other hand, studies in other parts of the world reveal a different meaning for the operation. For example, Béhague (2002) examined the meaning of Caesarean operations in Brazil and explored the reasons for women's preferences for Caesarean section births in Pelotas. She argues that women strategize and appropriate both medical knowledge and the technology of Caesarean sections as a creative form of responding to the economic, cultural and ideological system in which they find themselves. In a sense, demanding a Caesarean is also about demanding a better deal from the health care system. It is not surprising, then, that women are demanding the operation in ever larger numbers. Béhague (2002) argues that, for some women, the effort to medicalize the birth process represents a practical solution to problems found within the medical system itself. Thus, a procedure which some enlightened practitioners are seeking to reduce in the 'West' is gaining in popularity in other parts of the world because of what it signifies about one's lifestyle and as a way of increasing the medical attention one gets in conditions of medical scarcity. Postmodern approaches to the study of health care and society would delight in exploring such disparities and curiosities.

A further feature of postmodernism that deserves comment is how it allows us to think in new ways about familiar phenomena in such a way as to defamiliarize it and make it strange. This enables fresh insights to be gained. To illustrate this, let us forget for a moment that illness is somehow undesirable and think about the ways in which it is perhaps enjoyable. To deal with this, we can draw our theoretical position from Bakhtinian literary theory and encompass the interplay of different, apparently contradictory strands of illness experience within a dialectical model. This will help us establish a niche for these enigmatic and under-explored issues. Increasingly, as a

growing corpus of personal accounts testifies, it is becoming clear that a variety of experiences of enlightenment, transfiguration or aesthetic production can be detected in illness experience. Narrations of the experience of illness do not always describe it as unremittingly painful and may contain moments of comfort, positive transformation and even pleasure.

Whereas it may seem paradoxical to assert that illness may be pleasurable, it is clear that this is not a new idea to students of the area. A close reading of many of the classic texts of medical sociology and psychology reveals that pleasures are lurking just beneath the surface of illness. Talcott Parsons' (1951) concept of the sick role involved a legitimate release from the workaday obligations of the person's other roles and an opportunity, if not an obligation, to seek out nurturing and restorative experiences with health professionals. Gerhardt (1989) commented that the sick role is a kind of 'niche in the social system where the incapacitated may withdraw while attempting to mend their fences, with the help of the medical profession' (p. 15). Being a good patient may even be about putting on a token show of healthiness – bearing up well or being brave, for example. In another classic from the 1950s, Isobel Menzies Lyth (1988), in a psychoanalytically flavoured evocation of hospital life, saw the libido at work eroticizing the encounters between staff and patients.

Recent texts on the body and illness also repay an examination. Apparently for some authors there exists what Gillian Rose (1995) calls a state of 'accentuated being' afforded by illness. In academic life, illness experience that at an everyday level may be painful, debilitating or humiliating is a source of much storytelling (Frank 1995). As Arthur Frank (1997) puts it, there is an 'awesomeness' to accounts of the experience of illness which perhaps modifies how the experience itself is encoded and communicated. There is thus a dialectical interplay between pain and its amelioration. Our mention of the work of Bakhtin in this context is not capricious; he is apposite because he not only had much to say on dialogues and dialectics, but also about the grotesque and subversive aspects of the body. For Bakhtin (1973, 1981, 1984a,b), the grotesque body is a central feature of a topsy-turvy world which interrogates our familiar, stable world and questions its authoritarian monism. The grotesque body offers a symbolic subversion of the 'real' world and questions the cultural authority of official versions of the world with various alternative carnivalesque postulations. The phenomenon of carnival was central to Bakhtin's thought, for it was at these festivals throughout Europe in the Middle Ages and the Renaissance that the hierarchies of authority were temporarily challenged and inverted and the gross, profane and scatological aspects of the human condition were celebrated. Likewise, the grotesque, suffering body creates a 'gap' in the fabric of society and makes the 'body' less certain, homely or defined (Holquist and Clark 1984). The vulgarity of the grotesque body lies in its openness to the world. Illness, assault and modification tend to disrupt the body's envelope, puncture it, slit it, redefine its shape and its secretions (Pitts 1988). This *liminality*, or state of transition between health and illness, invites new sensations, experiences and identities. Biomedical accounts that stress the physiological aspects of disease can never exhaustively specify what the experience will be. Despite the discourses which emphasize the dire, desolate and agonizing aspects of illness, there are nevertheless possibilities for retrieving benefits, advantages and even pleasures from the experience. Furthermore, as Bakhtin (1986) would emphasize, 'I must find

myself in another by finding another in myself' (p. 63). This highlights how these experiences themselves can be seen as interconnected with the social context where they are occasioned, constructed, interpreted, cared for and healed.

Although pain and illness anchor us in our bodies, they also highlight the way that symptoms are not just obdurately there; they are often performed. Clearly, this can be seen in the great medical demonstrations of the late nineteenth century where prominent specialists displayed their patients' symptoms and cures before an audience. Most famously, Jean Martin Charcot demonstrated his cases of hysteria (Showalter 1987), but we can find less celebrated cases where an appropriate display of symptoms yields an identifiable payoff. In the present, community nurses speak of 'social ulcers' – that is, where isolated elderly clients cultivate their wounds so as to facilitate contact with the nurse (Carnegie 1994; Nesselroth and Gahtan 2000).

On the one hand, the display of illness and disability marks one as a person who is defined through the body (Seymour 1998); on the other, Bakhtin reminds us that the grotesque attributes of the body – which may well emerge in sickness – make identity ambiguous, multiple and marginal and it is to these possibilities for novel, sociohistorical productions of bodily experience to which we now turn. Central to grotesque realism is the principle of degradation, 'the lowering of all that is high, spiritual, ideal, abstract . . . to the material level, to the sphere of earth and body in their indissoluble unity' (Seymour 1998, pp. 19–20).

Western medicine has tended to focus on the biologically based causal mechanisms of illness. Moreover, it has tended to proceed on the assumption that the systems and organs of the body can be treated in relative isolation. The successful 'transplant' – the jewel in the crown of scientific medicine – is predicated on the notion that many of the body's parts are interchangeable between certain individuals. Generally, a further assumption is that the technologies of health care are separate and morally neutral entities that humans can use to shape their experience of the world for the better. These ideas have been problematized by postmodernism.

There are contradictory tendencies in medicine. At the same time as there is a growing interest in evidence-based practice, with the assumption that there can be a universal standard of evidence, there is the so-called postmodernization of general practitioners (Clayton 2002). This describes an increasing tendency on the part of practitioners not to rely on formal, scientifically derived knowledge, but on 'clinical legitimacy', whereby treatments are selected that appear to work for that particular patient. Thus, we see GPs referring their patients to complementary therapists, for example. There are also powerful voices calling for a renewed vision of medicine as an art of healing rather than a science, for example, while others (e.g. Eastwood 2000) strengthen their call for a greater reliance on science. Hence, even in the era of evidence-based practice, there are signs that not everyone is singing from the same song sheet.

Within postmodern approaches to health and illness, the familiar divisions between mind and body, culture and nature are blurred. It becomes possible to see diseases as somehow more profoundly linked with culture. Helman (1994) makes the point when he describes culture-bound disorders, where particular organs are preferential for particular cultures. In France, there is the *crise de foie* (liver), whereas in Iran it is *narahatiye qalb* or heart distress. Britain prefers disorders of the bowel and,

as Clayton (2002) argues, the organ of choice for women in Australia would be the breast. She speculates whether breast cancer is the manifestation of a society's obsession with stereotypical femininity. These links between culture and disease go beyond the familiar modernist medical concern between, say, smoking and lung cancer or diet and heart disease. Here, disease is seen as a kind of manifestation of culture.

Indeed, postmodernism invites us to be sceptical of the very symptoms we see in patients. Baudrillard (1983) says: 'For if any symptom can be "produced", and can no longer be accepted as a fact of nature, then every illness may be considered simulatable and simulated, and medicine loses its meaning since it only knows how to treat "true" illnesses by their objective causes' (p. 5). Clayton (2002) goes on to say: 'If subjectivity is in a continual state of flux, the body and mind are unstable referents. Therefore, the body as a site of experiential metamorphic production is worthy of further investigation' (p. 840). Thus, the meanings of symptoms and signs of the kind that previous generations of practitioners have been taught to recognize as a particular kind of disease may not be sufficient to make sense of the maladies of the twenty-first century. The past decade has seen a burgeoning of different kinds of health problem centred on immunity or some kind of ill-defined relationship between mind and body such as chronic fatigue syndrome, attention deficit hyperactivity disorder, depression or dissociative disorders. The grand illnesses of the past – tuberculosis, diphtheria, scarlet fever and the like – have been eclipsed by more complex syndromes with far less obvious aetiology.

As this chapter draws to a close, it is perhaps appropriate to ask what a postmodern approach to health care might look like. In this we are guided by the comments of Derrida (2001) about the humanities of tomorrow and a further commentary by Peters (2002) about the applicability of these to health care, in particular nursing. Derrida provides a list of seven programmatic statements as to how he would like to see the humanities disciplines developing, and it is to these we turn to see what implications postmodernism has for health care.

1) These new humanities would treat the history of man [sic], the idea, the figure, the notion of 'what is proper to man' . . . The most urgent guiding thread here would be the problematization . . . of those powerful judicial performatives that have given shape to this modern history of this humanity of man . . . on the other hand, the Declaration of the Rights of Man – and of course woman . . . and on the other hand, the concept of crimes against humanity, which since the end of the Second World War has modified the geopolitical field of international law . . .

2) These new humanities would treat, in the same style, the history of democracy and the idea of sovereignty. The deconstruction of this concept of sovereignty would touch not only on international law, the limits of the nation state, and of its supposed sovereignty, but also on the use made of them in judicio-political discourses concerning the relationship between what is called man and woman.

3) These new humanities would treat, in the same style, our history of 'professing', of the 'profession', and of the professoriat, a history articulated with that of the premises or presuppositions . . . of work and of the worldwide-ised

confession, there where it goes beyond the sovereignty of the Head of State, the nation state or even of the 'people' in a democracy. An immense problem: how to disassociate democracy from citizenship, from the nation state and from the theological idea of sovereignty, even the sovereignty of the people?

(Derrida 2001, pp. 241–4)

Let us pause for a moment and consider some of the implications of these statements for the health care disciplines. The concerns about government, jurisprudence and sovereignty here have, as Peters (2002) reminds us, a direct relevance to health care in the UK at least. Debates about refugees, asylum seekers and immigration have implications for how health is managed in the UK, and the increasing role of private sector finance in the health service invites concerns about the protection of the public sphere and the encroachment of market values into health care. Peters (2002) notes also that scholars of health care may well find it productive to investigate the 'government of health', in relation to citizen rights and democracy, emphasizing political, historical and philosophical aspects. Moreover, we may wish to be concerned with the question of to what extent is health a right of the citizen and to what extent this is related to democracy. In addition, it might be appropriate to ask which medical and commercial interests have most to gain from the privatization process. Moreover, how will the increasing introduction of market forces into health affect the relationship between patients and professionals? The concern over global health problems such as HIV or the scare over severe acute respiratory syndrome (SARS) in 2003 highlight the fact that there are health care issues that transcend national or sovereign boundaries. How do we conceptualize and study the differences between the 'health rich' and the 'health poor' in the globalized health market? Peters adds a further question: 'To what extent in the era of globalization is the government of health passing from the state to the multinational corporation?' (Peters 2002, p. 56). Furthermore, we might ask about the effects of all this privatization of health care on the research process, the kinds of tests which are done, the drugs which are approved and the commercial interests at stake in health care research.

Returning to Derrida's programme, let us consider some more of his vision of the new humanities and the questions they raised for health care:

4) These new humanities would treat, in the same style, the history of literature. Not only what is commonly called the history of literatures or literature themselves, with the great question of its canons . . . but the history of the concept of literature, of the modern institution named literature, of its links with fiction and the performative force of the 'as if', of the concept of oeuvre, author, signature, national language, of its link with the right to say or not to say everything that founds both democracy and the idea of the unconditional sovereignty claimed by the university and within it by what is called . . . the humanities.

5) These new humanities would treat, in the same style, the history of profession, the profession of faith, professionalization, and the professoriat. The guiding thread could be, today, what is happening when the profession of faith of the professor, gives rise to a singular oeuvres, to other strategies of the 'as if' that are

events and that affect the very limits of the academic field or of the humanities. We are indeed witnessing the end of a certain figure of the professor and of his or her supposed authority, but I believe as now should be obvious, in a certain necessity of the professoriat.

6) These new humanities would thus finally treat, in the same style, but in the course of a formidable reversal, both critical and deconstructive, the history of the 'as if' and especially the history of this precious distinction between performative acts and constantive acts that seems to have been indispensable to us until now.

7) To the seventh point, which is not the seventh day, I finally arrive now. Or rather, I let perhaps arrive at the end, now, the very thing that, by arriving, by taking place, revolutionises, overturns and puts to rout the very authority that is attached, in the university, in the humanities: (i) to knowledge (or at least constantive language); (ii) to the profession or to the profession of faith (or at least to its model of performative language); (iii) to the mise en oeuvre, the putting to work, at least to the performative putting to work of the 'as if'.

(Derrida 2001, pp. 241–4)

In addition to these kinds of ambitions about the humanities of tomorrow, Derrida paints a picture of what he calls the university of the future, which he says must be unconditionally free in both formulating questions and in the right to say publicly what is required by investigating, knowing and thinking. It needs, in his view, to be free from the commercial and political pressures that inhabit a good deal of academic life at present. He sees the ideals as a place of critical (deconstructive) resistance against the ideas of the powerful and the dogmatic interest groups within society. This resistance, this civil disobedience, is best expressed, in his view, through these new humanities that he outlined in the seven points above. These humanities are specified in a rather quaint manner, redolent of classical or Enlightenment ideas about academic freedom. The crucial difference, he sees, is that these studies must be deconstructed beforehand. Derrida's model of the new humanities is a profession of faith (*profession du foi*) of someone who performs the profession of professor. The question he asks is: what does it mean to profess (*professer*)? To reply to this question, Derrida tentatively accepts Austin's division of speech acts into constantive and performative, where constantive language is about things that are true and perfomative language is concerned with the performance itself. In Derrida's model, profession should not be constantive, but performative, because it is a work (*oeuvre*) itself, hence not in a final form.

However, according to Derrida, it is also necessary to ask the question of what is work (*travail*). The starting thought is: 'How the end of work was at the beginning of the world'. The term 'the end of work' is taken from the title of Rifkin's (1995) book *The End of Work*, and is connected with 'mondialation' (Derrida prefers this term to 'globalization'). Derrida's reading of Rifkin's book leads him to suppose that there has been a new revolution, 'moving us to the edge of a workerless world'. He claims that technological upheaval has occurred not only through cyberspace, microcomputing, cellular telephones and robotics, but by layoffs of millions of workers, including 'underpaid part-timers' at universities.

Let us pause for a moment and think about how some of this relates to the position in health care: the deskilling and deprofessionalization of many care tasks and the increasing reliance on voluntary and charitable labour to perform the more labour-intensive tasks of care; the loss of transport to clinics for elderly and infirm people, the difficulty in obtaining respite care and the waiting lists for many commonly required services are aspects of this. Discussion of the professoriat, and the issue of professing knowledge, is particularly apposite in health care too, for as Peters (2002) reminds us, the development of courses in nursing, physiotherapy, occupational therapy and audiology in universities means that there are new cadres of academics growing and developing careers in these professions. Equally, some of the traditional professions such as medicine have come under increasing suspicion. Peters sees one of the important tasks at stake here to be the development of a methodological self-reflection to theorize the relations of power in the teaching and practice of health care.

Derrida's keenness to break down the distinction between matters which are constantive (i.e. they make claims to the true, correct or verifiable depiction of existing states of affairs) and those which are performative (i.e. concerned with performance, presentation and doing) has implications for health care research and health care practice. If we cannot readily make the distinction between truth and doing, this means that there must be much greater attention to how health care is done in practice. Scholars such as Nicholas Fox (1993) and Marc Berg (1999) have provided sensitive, reflexive evocations of the use of technology in illness, suffering and care. When we perform operations upon patients, and store their data in electronic systems, this may have important implications for how we think about them. Whereas we cannot fully address these questions here, perhaps Derrida's most important claim is that to understand health care we need to make sense of the philosophy, politics and history behind it.

Derrida is also keen to suggest ways of thinking in universities and in the new humanities. As far as he is concerned, the university must be performative and this performativity must be 'as if' (*als ob*). This 'as if' is not an invitation to a fiction of possible futures. Instead, it takes into consideration the hypothetical or provisional nature of deconstruction. The humanities, he says, will have to study and analyse the concepts that they themselves introduced in their own historical construction. That is, Derridean philosophy invites us to become more fully reflexive, and understand how our own tools are involved in making the history of our disciplines and in creating our findings.

References

Abma, T.A. (1998) *The Art of Being Responsive to Differences*. Video presented to the AREA Annual Conference, San Diego, CA, April.

Abma, T.A. (2002) Emerging narrative forms of knowledge representation in the health sciences: two texts in a postmodern context, *Qualitative Health Research*, 12(1): 5–27.

Allen, D.G. (1995) Hermeneutics: philosophical traditions and nursing practice research, *Nursing Science Quarterly*, 8(4): 174–82.

Atkins, P. (2003) *Galileo's Finger: Ten Great Ideas of Science*. Buckingham: Open University Press.

Austin, J.L. (1962) *How To Do Things with Words*. Oxford: Clarendon Press.

Bakhtin, M.M. (writing as V.N. Voloshinov) (1973) *Marxism and the Philosophy of Language* (translated by L. Matejka and J.R. Titunik). New York: Seminar Press.

Bakhtin, M.M. (1981) *The Dialogic Imagination* (translated by C. Emerson and M. Holquist). Austin, TX: University of Texas Press.

Bakhtin, M.M. (1984a) *Rabelais and His World* (translated by H. Iswolsky). Cambridge, MA: MIT Press.

Bakhtin, M.M. (1984b) *Problems of Dostoyevsky's Poetics* (translated by C. Emerson). Minneapolis, MN: University of Minnesota Press.

Bakhtin, M.M. (1986) The problem of speech genres, in C. Emerson and M. Holquist (eds) *Speech Genres and Other Late Essays* (translated by V.W. McGee). Austin, TX: University of Texas Press.

Barone, T.E. (1997). Among the chosen: a collaborative educational (auto)biography, *Qualitative Inquiry*, 3(2): 222–36.

Baudrillard, J. (1983) The Precession of Simulacra, in J. Fleming and S. Lotringer (eds) *Simulations* (translated by P. Foss, P. Patton and P. Beitchman). New York: Columbia University Press.

Baudrillard, J. (1990) *Fatal Strategies: Crystal Revenge*. London Pluto/Semiotexte.

Baudrillard, J. (1995) *The Gulf War Did Not Take Place*. Sydney, NSW: Power Publications.

Béhague, D.P. (2002) Beyond the simple economics of Caesarean section birthing: women's resistance to social inequality, *Culture, Medicine and Psychiatry*, 26(4): 473–507.

Berg, M. (1999) Patient care information systems and health care work: a sociotechnical approach, *International Journal of Medical Informatics*, 55: 87–101.

Beverley, J. (2000). Testimonio, subalternity, and narrative authority, in N.K. Denzin and Y.S. Lincoln (eds) *Handbook of Qualitative Research*. Thousand Oaks, CA: Sage.

Blumenfeld-Jones, D.S. (1995) Dance as a mode of representation, *Qualitative Inquiry*, 1(14): 391–401.

Boyne, R. (1992) *Foucault and Derrida*. London: Unwin Hyman.

Breggin, P. (2000) *Reclaiming Our Children: A Healing Solution for a Nation in Crisis*. Cambridge, MA: Perseus Books.

Britten, N. (1994) Patients' ideas about medicines: a qualitative study in a general practice population, *British Journal of General Practice*, 44: 465–8.

Carnegie, A. (1994) Leg ulcer care in the community, *Journal of Wound Care*, 8(4): 157–8.

Cheek, J. and Rudge, T. (1994) Nursing as textually mediated reality, *Nursing Inquiry*, 1(1): 15–22.

Clarke, L. (1996) The last post? Defending nursing against the postmodernist maze, *Journal of Psychiatric and Mental Health Nursing*, 3: 257–65.

Clayton, B. (2002) Rethinking postmodern maladies, *Current Sociology*, 50(6): 839–51.

Darbyshire, P. (1994) Reality bites: the theory and practice of nursing narratives, *Nursing Times*, 90(40): 31–3.

Deleuze, G. and Guattari, F. (1984) *Anti-Oedipus: Capitalism and Schizophrenia* (translated by R. Hurley, M. Seem and H.R. Lane). London: Athlone.

Denzin, N.K. (1999) Two-stepping in the '90s, *Qualitative Inquiry*, 5(4): 568–72.

Derrida, J. (1977) *Of Grammatology* (translated by G.C. Spivak). Baltimore, MD: Johns Hopkins University Press.

Derrida, J. (1978) *Writing and Differance*. London: Routledge.

Derrida, J. (2001) The future of the professions or the unconditional university (thanks to the 'humanities', what could take place tomorrow), in L. Simmons and H. Worth (eds) *Derrida Downunder*. Palmerston North, NZ: Dunmore Press.

Dougan, H.A.S. (1995) The role of the nurse, in P.I. Peattie and S. Walker (eds) *Understanding Nursing Care*, 4th edn. Edinburgh: Churchill Livingstone.

Eastwood, H. (2000) Complementary therapies: the appeal to general practitioners, *Medical Journal of Australia*, 173: 95–8.

Ellis, C. and Bocher, A.P. (2000) Authoethnography, personal narrative, reflexivity: researcher as subject, in N.K. Denzin and Y.S. Lincoln (eds) *Handbook of Qualitative Research*. Thousand Oaks, CA: Sage.

Falk, L. and Perron, M. (1995) The conversion of Père Version, in C.H. Gray (ed.) *The Cyborg Handbook*. New York: Routledge.

Fenwick, J., Gamble, J. and Mawson, J. (2003) Women's experiences of caesarean section and vaginal birth after caesarean: a Birthrites initiative, *International Journal of Nursing Practice*, 9: 10–17.

Foucault, M. (1965) *Madness and Civilisation*. New York: Random House.

Foucault, M. (1975) *The Birth of the Clinic: An Archaeology of Medical Perception*. New York: Vintage.

Fox, N.J. (1992) *The Social Meaning of Surgery*. Philadelphia, PA: Open University Press.

Fox, N.J. (1993) *Postmodernism, Sociology and Health*. Toronto: University of Toronto Press.

Frank, A. (1995) *The Wounded Storyteller: Body, Illness and Ethics*. Chicago, IL: University of Chicago Press.

Frank, A. (1997) Narrative witness to bodies: a response to Alan Radley, *Body and Society*, 3(3): 103–9.

Gerhardt, U. (1989) *Ideas about Illness: An Intellectual and Political History of Medical Sociology*. London: Macmillan.

Glesne, G. (1997) That rare feeling: re-presenting research through poetic transcription, *Qualitative Inquiry*, 3(2): 202–21.

Green, J. and Britten, N. (1998) Qualitative research and evidence based medicine, *British Medical Journal*, 316: 1230–2.

Grice, H.P. (1975) Logic and conversation, in P. Cole and J.P. Morgan (eds) *Syntax and Semantics 3: Speech Acts*. New York: Academic Press.

Gurevitz, D. (1997) *Postmodernism, Culture and Literature at the End of the 20th Century*. Tel Aviv: Dvir.

Held, B.S. (2002) The tyranny of the positive attitude in America: observations and speculations, *International Journal of Clinical Psychology*, 58(9): 965–91.

Helman, C.G. (1994) *Culture, Health and Illness*. Oxford: Butterworth Heinemann.

Henderson, V. (1966) *The Nature of Nursing*. London: Collier Macmillan.

Hewett, G. (1994) '*Just a Part of Me': Men's Reflections on Chronic Asthma*. Occasional Papers in Sociology and Social Policy. London: South Bank University.

Hollinger, R. (1994) *Postmodernism and the Social Sciences*. London: Sage.

Holquist, M. and Clark, K. (1984) *Mikhail Bakhtin*. Cambridge, MA: Harvard University Press.

hooks, b. (1990) *Yearning: Race, Gender, and Cultural Politics*. Boston, MA: South End.

Hull, F.M. and Marshall, T. (1987) Sources of information about new drugs and attitudes towards drug prescribing: an international study of differences between primary care physicians, *Family Practitioner*, 4: 123–8.

Katon, W. and Kleinman, A. (1981) Doctor–patient negotiation and other social science strategies in patient care, in L. Eisenberg and A. Kleinman (eds) *The Relevance of Social Science to Medicine*. Dordrecht: Reidel.

Kivnick, H.Q. (1996) Remembering and being remembered: the reciprocity of psychological legacy, *Generations: Journal of the American Society on Aging*, 20(3): 49–53.

Lacan, J. (1977) *Écrits* (translated by A. Sheridan). London: Tavistock.

Lapidus, I.M. (1996) Photo essay, *Women's Studies*, 25: 363–70.

Lather, P. and Smithies, C. (1997) *Troubling the Angels: Women Living with HIV/AIDS*, Boulder, CO: Westview.

Laurence, J. and McCallum, D. (1998) The myth or reality of attention deficit hyperactivity disorder: a genealogical approach, *Discourse: Studies in the Cultural Politics of Education*, 19(2): 183–200.

Lee-Treweek, G. (2002) Trust in complementary medicine: the case of cranial osteopathy, *Sociological Review*, 50(1): 48–68.

Lemert, C. (1990) The uses of French structuralisms in sociology, in G. Ritzer (ed.) *Frontiers of Social Theory: The New Syntheses*. New York: Columbia University Press.

Lewis, B. (2000) Psychiatry and postmodern theory, *Journal of Medical Humanities*, 21(2): 71–84.

Lister, P. (1997) The art of nursing in a postmodern context, *Journal of Advanced Nursing*, 25: 38–44.

Lyotard, J.-F. (1984) *The Postmodern Condition: A Report on Knowledge* (translated by G. Bennington and B. Massumi). Manchester: Manchester University Press.

Mansfield, N. (2000) *Subjectivity: Theories of the Self from Freud to Haraway*. St Leonards, NSW: Allen & Unwin.

Maynard, D. (1991) The perspective display series and the delivery of diagnostic news, in D. Boden and D.H. Zimmerman (eds) *Talk and Social Structure*. Cambridge: Polity Press.

Menzies Lyth, I. (1988) *Containing Anxiety in Institutions: Selected Essays*, Vol. 1. London: Free Association Books.

Mienczakowski, J.E. (1995) The theatre of ethnography: the reconstruction of ethnography into theatre with an emancipatory potential, *Qualitative Inquiry*, 1: 360–75.

Mishler, E.G. (1984) *The Discourse of Medicine: Dialectics of Medical Interviews*. Norwood, NJ: Ablex.

Morgan, G. (1986) *Images of Organisation*. London: Sage.

Nesselroth, S.M. and Gahtan, V. (2000) Management of pressure ulcers in the home care setting, *Home Healthcare Consultant*, 7(4): 34–42.

Norris, J.R. (1997) Meaning through form: alternative modes of knowledge representation, in J.M. Morse (ed.) *Completing a Qualitative Project: Details and Dialogue*. Thousand Oaks, CA: Sage.

Osman, L.M., Russell, I.T., Friend, J.A.R., Legge, J.S. and Douglas, J.G. (1993) Predicting patient attitudes to asthma medication, *Thorax*, 48: 827–30.

Parker, I., Georgaca, E., Harper, D., McLaughlin, T. and Stowell-Smith, M. (1995) *Deconstructing Psychopathology*, London: Sage.

Parsons, T. (1951) *The Social System*. London: Routledge & Kegan Paul.

Pellegrino, E. (1979) *Humanism and the Physician*. Knoxville, TN: University of Tennessee Press.

Peplau, H.E. (1952) *Interpersonal Relations in Nursing*. New York: G.P. Putnam.

Peters, M. (2002) Derrida and the tasks for the new humanities: postmodern nursing and the culture wars, *Nursing Philosophy*, 3: 47–57.

Pfohl, S. (1992) *Death at the Parasite Cafe: Social Science (Fiction) and the Postmodern*. Basingstoke: Macmillan.

Pitts, V.L. (1988) Reclaiming the female body: embodied identity work, resistance and the grotesque, *Body and Society*, 4(3): 67–84.

Randi, J. (1992) *Conjuring*. New York: St. Martin's Press.

Richardson, L. (1993) Poetics, dramatics and transgressive validity: the case of the skipped line, *The Sociological Quarterly*, 34(4): 695–710.

Rifkin, J. (1995) *The End of Work: The Decline of the Global Labor Force and the Dawn of the Post-Market Era*. New York: J.P. Tarcher.

Ritzer, G. (1992) *Sociological Theory*. New York: McGraw-Hill.

Rose, G. (1995) *Love's Work*. London: Chatto & Windus.

Rose, N. (1990) *Governing the Soul: The Shaping of the Private Self.* London: Routledge.

Rose, N. (1996) Psychiatry as political science: advanced liberalism and the administration of risk, *History of Human Sciences,* 9(2): 1–23.

Sarup, M. (1988) *An Introduction to Post-Structuralism and Post-Modernism.* Hemel Hempstead: Harvester Wheatsheaf,

Scannell, P., Schlesinger, P. and Sparks, C. (eds) (1992) *Culture and Power: A Media, Culture and Society Reader.* London: Sage.

Searle, J. (1969) *Speech Acts: An Essay in the Philosophy of Language.* London: Cambridge University Press.

Schegloff, E.A. (1997) Whose text? Whose context?, *Discourse and Society,* 8(2): 165–88.

Seymour, W. (1998) *Remaking the Body: Rehabilitation and Change.* London: Routledge.

Showalter, E. (1987) *The Female Malady.* London: Virago.

Spitzer, A. (1998) Nursing in the health care system of the postmodern world: crossroads, paradoxes and complexity, *Journal of Advanced Nursing,* 28(1): 164–71.

Sutherland Society (2001) Cranial osteopathy (http://www.cranial.org.uk).

10

Philosophy and research design in practice

Introduction

This chapter considers how we might conceptualize knowledge in health care and how researchers might go about the knowledge generation process. Rather than simply rehearse a set of methodological guidelines about how research might be better done if researchers were aware of philosophical issues, we will attempt to show how different kinds of epistemologies and approaches to knowledge exist in different branches of the health care disciplines. There are a variety of growths in the health care garden, many of which co-exist comfortably, yet which appear to be structured in dominance according to issues such as prestige, status, fashion and finances. In addition, different health care disciplines have conceptualized the kinds of knowledge they are based on differently. In contrast to the enthusiasm for randomized controlled clinical trials in medicine, nursing has a well-known typology originated by Carper (1978) that divides knowledge into empirical, ethical, personal and aesthetic knowledge; the notion of socio-political knowledge was added by White (1995). We will discuss how different conceptions of knowledge, different values and different positions in the socio-political framework might yield different kinds of research questions and might predispose actors towards differing research methods. The knowledge desired by a community mental health nurse seeing an isolated elderly client may be different from that desired by a drug company, or a lecturer on a health studies programme.

It is also perhaps important to consider how knowledge is represented by practitioners, yet as we shall see, expertise has been extremely difficult to characterize. Generally, more tacit knowledge is deployed by expert practitioners, and we will examine how this might lead to the formulation of research questions and strategies for interrogating existing research knowledge. We shall also consider what practical implications there are in adopting a philosophical turn of mind for health care researchers and practitioners. We shall show how this offers powerful intellectual tools for making sense of the medical and social world, evaluating theories, research designs and methods and even critically appraising completed studies.

There are a variety of practical and financial issues in promoting and implementing research, and the policies adopted by research councils, government bodies and

industry will be crucial in determining the kinds of knowledge which emerge from the research community. These foci of concern may have an impact on the kind of philosophy of science we adopt in trying to make sense of research. On the way to becoming practitioners and researchers, students will thus need to acquire a sense of why and how research and knowledge are paid for and how economic considerations may inform the choice of research topic, research personnel and even, perhaps, the outcome of research in the industrialized economies of the West. Some of the issues described in this book so far might be useful to help understand this process.

Ways of knowing: nursing and beyond

The idea that there are different levels or 'ways of knowing' has a long pedigree in nursing. For the past 50 years or so, nursing scholars have tried to define what it is that nursing does, and how this relates to the kind of knowledge derived and used by nurses in their everyday practice. Peplau's (1952) generative work sought to redefine nursing as a primarily interpersonal discipline and, more recently, a famous taxonomy of 'ways of knowing in nursing' was developed (Carper 1978). This framework, where knowledge is seen as involving four kinds of 'knowing', has been influential in nursing for nearly a quarter of a century at the time of writing: these are empirical, ethical, aesthetic and personal knowledge. This point in the development of the profession represented a move away from its positivistic roots. Let us describe these four kinds of knowledge in more detail.

Empirical knowledge corresponds to the legitimized, scientific version of what the world consists of and how it can be operated upon. Like many conventional accounts of science that we have encountered in this volume, it is aimed at developing general laws, principles and theories so as to explain, describe and predict phenomena in nursing. It might involve the usual suspects in the education of health professionals – anatomy, physiology and pharmacology – as well as the growing body of scientific knowledge in general. In the present day, it might correspond to the kinds of scientifically derived knowledge, rich in quantification and double-blind randomized controlled designs, which go to make up the canon of evidence-based practice as it is currently conceived.

Ethical or *moral knowledge* concerns ethical issues in nursing and focuses on issues of duty and responsibility. This involves knowledge of codes of conduct and the ability to distinguish ethical issues and appreciate the moral dimensions of an issue. This way of knowing comprises the understanding and the ability to apply moral and ethical frameworks to complex situations requiring moral insight and judgement. It encompasses valuing, clarifying and advocacy on behalf of the client, while acknowledging that they have the human freedom, will and knowledge to make decisions on their own behalf. This may also involve awareness of the way that some moral dilemmas cannot easily be solved. It might, moreover, be possible to subsume political and spiritual knowledge under this heading, as well as knowledge concerning the larger-scale contribution to human welfare made by a health care intervention.

Personal knowledge involves self-understanding and is 'concerned with the knowing, encountering, and actualizing the concrete, individual self' (Carper 1978, p. 18). In this view, knowing oneself makes it possible to use the self therapeutically. Personal

knowledge involves the capacity to 'access one's own feeling life – one's range of emotions: the capacity instantly to effect discriminations among the feelings and, eventually, to label them, to enmesh them in symbolic codes, e.g. language, touch, writing to draw upon them as a means of understanding and guiding one's behaviour' (Gardner 1983, p. 239).

Johns (1995a) describes the *aesthetic way of knowing* as the 'intuitive grasp of and response to a clinical situation' (p. 228). Aesthetics also includes the expressive aspect of nursing and comprises knowledge gained through the 'subjective acquaintance' of direct experience and becomes visible in the craft skills through which the nurse uses self on behalf of the individual (Carper 1978, p. 16). Aesthetic knowing involves the synthesis and expression of all of the patterns of nursing knowledge and, of necessity, will be unique to each nurse. It also necessitates the recognition of unique details and particulars rather than the universal, and is based around integration, synthesis, perception, intuition, creativity and empathy. Aesthetic knowing requires a process of engagement, interpretation and envisioning. This may even appear in the informal language of health care. A friend of one of the authors (B.B.) described how in wound care a wound might look 'sweet'. On exploration of this term, it appeared that this was to do with how likely the wound was to heal satisfactorily. It might appear smaller from day to day, less 'sloughy' and less red around the edges. It might have new granulations around the edge closing in. A 'sweet' wound, however, might still look gruesome to the uninitiated.

This typology of ways of knowing has been enhanced by the addition of a fifth kind. White (1995) argues that socio-political knowledge merits a category of its own. This relates to the context of nursing and addresses the context of the people involved, including the nurse and the client, as well as the profession. This involves both society's understanding of nursing and nursing's understanding of society and its politics. Socio-political knowing includes a focus on whose views are being heard and whose are being silenced. In practice, it involves exposing, exploring, transforming, transposing and critically analysing.

The identification of these forms of knowledge by Carper and White has led to a considerable degree of reflection in nursing on the kinds of knowledge that nurses use and the way that knowledge informs practice. The dominance of medicine in health care studies has perhaps resulted in it having a rather static view of its science, philosophy and practice, as if the knowledge from the laboratory and the clinical trial were unproblematically translatable to consulting room. This has not developed to anything like the same extent in nursing, where, despite the proliferation of models and protocols, the field has been characterized by much greater diversity and a greater hunger for ideas from other disciplines. This tendency is not unique to nursing. It may be possible to detect it in occupational therapy, too, especially as this has recently moved to being a more academically based subject and has carved out roles for itself in counselling, therapeutic and forensic contexts. In addition, the training curricula of a variety of professions allied to medicine are in the process of being modified so as to include more social, interpersonal and communication-related concerns. These changes in the organization of education and training cannot help but shift the knowledge bases and world-views of the professions concerned.

This tendency to focus on the interpersonal aspects of the health care encounter is often found hand in hand with a more interpretive stance in relation to the issue of how we make sense of what takes place in health care. Lathlean and Vaughan (1994) argue that this 'interpretative school' of scholarship in nursing has provided the profession with considerable insight into the nature of its practice. The 'interpretative school' is usually dated from the pioneering work of Benner (1984) and Benner and Wrubel (1989), but in some ways its origins go back much further, possibly even to Florence Nightingale herself. She was especially concerned with the 'moral qualities' of the nurse, which, in a rather quaint nineteenth-century idiom, may well have been addressing similar issues to those concerned today with the interpretive and interpersonal aspects of nursing.

Nursing, then, is a useful example because it illustrates the epistemological drift that has overtaken some of the health care professions. This drift away from positivism – or at least what its detractors believe positivism to be – has confronted health care scholars with the need to place their understanding of what they do on other footings. In tandem with this epistemological drift, then, it is possible to detect commitments on the part of nursing scholars that emphasize issues which are profoundly philosophical. In addition to the layers of knowledge or ways of knowing outlined by Carper above, some equally puzzling dilemmas remain to be negotiated. In illustrating this we will remain with the example of nursing because that is the one that has been most fully theorized, but the remarks may well apply to other health care disciplines.

One difficult thing to learn in the process of becoming a health care practitioner is that health care – at least according to some of its theorists – is not essentially concerned with tasks but with judgement. To simply learn how to do tasks is to only learn enabling skills (Benner 1982). Nursing, for instance, is believed to be a context-bound activity and one can only learn to be an interpretative nurse by entering into the world of the client. This, then, confronts the practitioner or researcher with a need to develop expertise as a phenomenologist. To be both an effective practitioner and an effective researcher it is desirable to be able to imagine what the world looks like from the point of view of the client and to understand how interpersonal processes have a role to play in facilitating the growth of understanding in particular ways. This area of expertise is different from, and sometimes sits uneasily with, the technical rationality of what Carper calls empirical knowing. However, in some cases, the kind of knowledge that derives from experience and understanding can have an equally valuable role to play in clinical contexts.

Layers of knowledge, layers of experience and new social objects

Let us illustrate this with the example of violence and the use of restraint in mental health contexts. This is a notoriously fraught area and was the subject of a study by Bonner et al. (2002), who interviewed both staff and clients who had been involved in incidents of this kind. In describing the run up to these incidents, clients often described some sort of failed communication prior to the outburst. For example: 'I got very angry because they wouldn't listen to what I was trying to tell them. Telling them that I needed help, wanted to hurt myself . . . it was horrible, I never want it to happen again' (Bonner et al. 2002, p. 468). Once incidents had taken place, there was

sometimes a good deal of bitterness about how the event had been handled. 'I didn't feel like a human being, I felt like I was just a number, I thought they were going to kill me' (p. 468). The incidents also left their mark on the staff. 'It's the frustration of not meeting her needs, although I try' (p. 469). And, after a particularly noteworthy incident in which a patient armed with a weapon had mounted an attack on staff, one nurse recounted the following story:

> I was terrified. I've never been so scared in all my life. The incident happened at 13.30. I didn't sit down until 16.20. I had wet myself because I was so terrified and I couldn't go home to change my trousers. The duty senior nurse wouldn't let me go because she said that she couldn't find a free trained member of staff throughout the entire hospital. I didn't want to tell her or anybody else that I'd wet myself so I had to stay in my wet trousers until the end of the shift.
>
> (Bonner *et al.* 2002, p. 469)

In addition, both patients and nurses disclosed that the events had brought back memories of earlier traumatic or violent incidents, such as being raped.

From the point of view of practical applications, although this study was small in scale and included only six incidents, it has yielded a number of implications for research and practice. Staff and patients expressed the importance of adequate debriefing – being able to talk through the incident afterwards was especially appreciated by patients who had been restrained. It also highlights the practical benefits of being able to spot the signs of an impending incident before it happens, especially given that patients claimed to have made it clear that they were going to become angry. In addition to these practical benefits that come from attempts to understand, there are some more philosophically oriented issues that this raised. For example, the way that everyday events are opportunities to do some sort of investigation, no matter how difficult they may be. As Hans Gerth and C. Wright Mills (1964) observed in *Character and Social Structure*, 'Problems of the nature of human nature are raised most urgently when the life-routines of a society are disturbed, when men are alienated from their social roles in such a way as to open themselves up for new insight' (p. xiii). These disjunctures in social reality tell us something important about the kind of world we are embedded in as researchers, patients and practitioners. Individual thoughts, feelings and experiences gain their meaning from the parts they play in larger-scale social wholes. Moreover, this kind of incident and the research that has been done on it shows how the close observation of regrettable everyday events can yield new insights into the nature of trauma. Bonner *et al.* (2002) note that their research has yielded a unique observation about the nature of trauma. The experience of restraint incidents in the hospital involved a traumatic re-experiencing of previous violent events for some of their patients and, more intriguingly, also for some of the staff. This shows how, with an eye for detail, the observation of mundane phenomena can open up new lines of enquiry. Once we have a theory, no matter how incompletely formed, we can use it to identify other observations of a similar kind. As Karl Popper ([1935] 1959) noted, theory is 'the net which we throw out in order to catch the world – to rationalize, explain, and dominate it' (p. 26).

Even where there is some agreement between staff and patients as to what is important and what matters, there can still be some important discrepancies. Holden and Smart (1999) were interested in what 'adds value' to the experience of being an 'emergency room' patient. They found that whereas issues such as waiting time, symptom relief, a caring and kind attitude on the part of staff and a diagnosis were all important to both staff and patients, waiting time was most important to patients but least important to staff. Thus, even when there was some agreement on the issues, there was a mismatch between patients' priorities and the perceptions of staff. The authors say that this justifies the use of waiting times as a performance indicator for emergency medicine. In this sense, then, a piece of research as ordinary as this can lead to policy changes in health care. Here, although the research itself is worthwhile, it is not methodologically or theoretically ambitious.

In the two examples above, we have discussed the entities 'patient' and 'staff' as if it was possible to tell the difference between the two, and as if these formed neatly bounded classes of people, as they clearly do in many classic studies of institutional life, for example by Goffman (1961). In terms of what is going on nowadays, of course, these very categories are blurring. Informally, we have noted that patients do jobs for each other on hospital wards that might once have been done by nurses. More officially, the present policy framework in the UK involves users being involved in service planning, research, needs assessment and in a helping role for one another as advocates. In any case, the use of the very term patient is being eclipsed by terms like 'user' or 'consumer'. This then prompts the possibility of reflection on what the social actors in health care are. Aspis (1997) reported some users who wanted to be called 'students' rather than clients. In addition, this kind of relationship creates new collective social objects as people get together to support each other (Aspis 1997). In addition, as consumers are encouraged to be more active in negotiating and organizing their care, new kinds of social body are unfolded. The new entrepreneurial patient, consumer, user or 'student' may well also find new ways of complaining about services that do not measure up to their new expectations. They may, as Abbott et al. (2001) discovered, be disappointed about the lack of information provided, they may be unclear about how their needs had been assessed and be unhappy about the lack of regular contact with health or social services personnel. So there are new sources of dissatisfaction and failure as well as new successes to be measured.

In addition, relatively new areas of concern have opened up. One example is the issue of disability and sexuality, where over the past few years increasing concern has been expressed by both carers and service users themselves. People with learning difficulties in particular have moved from a position where intimate relationships were treated with an unhappy mixture of disapproval and sterilization. Having intimate relationships while being disabled is complicated by the fact that people with disabilities often find themselves policed by caregivers and excluded from the range of informal and formal processes by which non-disabled people are socialized into intimate relationships and sexuality (Davies 2000). In addition, as Davies points out, once people with disabilities begin to see themselves as gay, lesbian, bisexual or transgendered, the whole situation becomes even more complex.

In the face of all this creation and recreation of people and identities, it is particularly useful to have a philosophically informed cast of mind as we examine these new

issues and movements. As researchers and practitioners in health care, we have a dual role both as observers and participants. The likelihood is that sooner or later we, too, will have health problems or disabilities that will involve us in being a client, patient or user. Philosophy does not necessarily give us a set of guidelines for understanding the world, but by confronting the different ideas and perspectives from thinkers, researchers, sufferers, healers and philosophers, we can perhaps make some headway.

Representing knowledge and becoming expert

Knowledge and how it is represented have been continuous themes throughout this book. We have attempted to address the diverse ways in which health professionals conceptualize the world. However, so far our account has been based largely on their written, drawn or photographed traces, what they write in textbooks or technical journals, and what is encoded in policy documents. In addition to this, it is also possible that practice itself, especially skilled practice, draws on different domains of knowledge and different ways of representing expertise which we have scarcely begun to characterize. To get a grip on this it is necessary to consider the processes involved in intuition and tacit knowledge. The intuitive aspects of skilled practice in health care are particularly difficult to study because they have been reduced in relevance under the technical rationality of the biomedical model. Yet health professionals, especially when they are experienced, may well use intuitive skills frequently. These skills enable practitioners to 'understand, to speak, and to cope skilfully with our everyday environment' (Dreyfus and Dreyfus 1985, p. xx). Because it is largely tacit, intuition is a nebulous form of knowledge that has not been studied extensively, as it cannot be explained or observed easily (Johns 1995b). In making sense of intuition, researchers have often turned to the work of Edmund Husserl (1859–1938), the originator of the phenomenological movement in Germany, who sought to interpret the inner spiritual and cognitive understandings of humans. In Husserl's formulation, the term 'intuiting' was central to phenomenology. Here, intuition involves 'logical insight based on careful consideration of representative examples: it is not second sight or inspiration' (Wilkes 1991, p. 233). Rew (1988, p. 150) identifies it as a 'higher form of vision'.

To place the notion of intuition into a framework that locates the kinds of skills found in health care, let us examine the work of Benner. Benner (1992) describes the progression of skill development in nursing, but it could equally well apply to other health professionals. It is proposed that skill levels develop from that of novice, to an advanced beginner stage, to a competent stage, to a proficient stage, to an expert stage. This typology was based on a model of skills acquisition developed by Dreyfus and Dreyfus, who believed that artificial intelligence, for example computer programs, was limited when it came to 'commonsense understanding' (Paterson 1991, p. 7). In Benner's account, as nurses acquire skills their thinking moves from reliance on abstract rules to reliance on past concrete experiences. As it does so, it undergoes a shift from rule-based analysis to intuition. The practitioners' perception changes from perceiving parts of a situation to the whole situation (Benner 1992). Dreyfus and Dreyfus (1985) suggest that novices use overly simple heuristic rules, while experts internalize their knowledge. This implies that domain experts are less able to explain their behaviour than novices. Warelow (1997, p. 1022) adds that

when nurses become experts and practise using intuition, their 'theory, practice and experienced wisdom . . .' work in harmony.

Dreyfus (1979) outlined six key aspects of intuition, which it is possible to identify. These are normally listed as if they were a kind of progression from the simplest to the more complicated, yet it is clear that they depend on one another and are closely interrelated. The first is pattern recognition, where relationships between a group of features within a particular context are perceived as a recognizable pattern. The second key aspect of intuitive judgement is similarity recognition, where the observer detects features which the situation or the person has with others. The third key aspect of intuition is commonsense understanding, which involves knowledge of the culture and language, and some sort of tacit grasp of what happens and what matters. The fourth aspect of intuition is skilled know-how, which is where one's body can carry out the task without consciously thinking, called 'embodied intelligence' by Paterson (1991, p.14). Some refer to this as 'brain-stem memory'. It seems that we are in automatic pilot, yet we are not performing mindlessly or mechanically. The fifth aspect of intuition is a sense of salience, which is where some features stand out in a situation as being more important than others. Finally, deliberative nationality involves comparing current situations with situations in the past, while considering the different perspectives and interpretations of the situations.

This progression of knowledge and practice – from the explicit procedural and technical knowledge acquired by the novice to the invisible exercise of skill on the part of the advanced practitioner – has meant that the sorts of knowledge representation involved in this kind of advanced practice have remained elusive. Indeed, many theorists have described it in somewhat mystical terms. Darling (1995, p. 16) describes intuition as 'the power of gaining knowledge without rational thought'. This notion of understanding that somehow occurs before or without reasoning appears to be widespread among writers on the subject. Schraeder and Fischer (1986) also say intuition is 'the immediate knowing of something without the conscious use of reason' (p. 161).

The sense of ineffability about the skilled practitioner's intuition and expertise is widely touted as being a key feature. The awareness involved in intuition is immediate and is a 'knowing in action' (Lumby 1991, p. 467). It is believed to be common to all people to the extent that it is 'a universal characteristic of human thought' (Rew 1988, p. 150). It is often expressed as a feeling or knowing and, despite the commonplace distinction that is drawn between reason and intuition, it is not necessarily in conflict with analytical reasoning. Schraeder and Fischer (1986) agree with Carl Jung that 'intuition is another dimension of knowing and is not in opposition to deductive or inductive reasoning' (p. 1). Indeed, intuition and analytical reasoning often work together (Benner and Tanner 1987).

Part of the appeal of these quasi-mystical accounts lies in the difficulty of specifying exactly what it is that experts do as they apply their obscurely represented knowledge so as to solve new practice problems creatively. Artificial intelligence theorists have struggled for many years with the problem of representing expertise in such a way as to enable it to be run on a computer. This is taken to suggest that there are parts of the creative process which defy automation. Moreover, some theorists, notably Dreyfus and Dreyfus (1985), warn of the mediocrity that arises from replacing too much of the human thought process with automation. The rule-governed,

programmable variety will never be as good as the intuitive version, it is argued. As Dreyfus and Dreyfus (1985) have argued in their classic critiques of traditional approaches to artificial intelligence, experts have a well-tuned sense of relevance that saves them from having to consider irrelevant aspects of the situation at hand. Computer chess-playing programs, for example, almost invariably proceed by considering a large number of moves, whereas the human chess expert – pretty evenly matched with a computer these days – tends to see patterns and possibilities in the game.

This, then, invites the problem of how people represent knowledge, which is one we have thought about periodically throughout this book. A reflective and scholarly stance on the part of readers will enable them to consider what kinds of knowledge are present in a given situation and think about how they are represented – is the knowledge implicit or explicit, traditional or postmodern, public or secret? This kind of literacy with knowledge, concepts and world-views is increasingly important in the current climate in health care with the vogue on both sides of the Atlantic for some form of evidence-based practice and the growing expectation that practitioners will be research literate. The kind of philosophical awareness that we have been illustrating and advocating throughout this book is one step on the way towards being able to make one's way through this new set of demands and apply philosophy in practical contexts.

The climate researchers encounter during their careers will also depend on the kinds of philosophies they adopt. At present, qualitative and interpretive researchers complain that they are disadvantaged when funding for research is dispensed and that the purse strings are loosened for those with a track record of quantitative research. An alignment with the more powerful interests in a given situation will very likely yield a different kind of experience than attempting to plough a less prestigious furrow. Thus, the old cliché 'That's a great idea, boss' may well apply in research and clinical practice as well.

The study of folk concepts: social representations

One way to fine-tune the thinking tools we have at our disposal is to look at those of other people and borrow from them. We have just discussed how difficult it is to characterize expertise, so to some extent this possibility doesn't look hopeful. However, there are a number of ways to study how thinking is done in everyday contexts. To illustrate this, let us look at one influential approach, namely that of social representations theory. Looking at concept formulations in their natural habitats as people go about their everyday tasks of making sense of the world, being ill or performing acts of healing, has frequently been used in the study of 'social representations'. Again, let us take a detour into the social sciences to see what the progenitors of this approach have been able to achieve in terms of examining the concepts that exist in everyday sense-making. The idea of social representations was originated in the 1950s by Moscovici (1976) to explain how a good deal of terminology from psychoanalysis had found its way into everyday culture in France. This tendency of everyday conversation to include terms from psychology and psychotherapy was also noted in California by Rosen (1977), in his book *Psychobabble*. In France in the 1950s,

Moscovici's original study used sources of data such as surveys, as well as church publications and women's magazines. There was a good deal of evidence that terms like 'repression' had become part of everyday vocabulary – people were using psychoanalysis to think about themselves and each other without appearing to do anything theoretical at all. This version of psychoanalysis, however, was a simplified one. Some terms like 'libido' had not found their way into the popular lexicon. The 'social representation' of psychoanalysis, then, is the simplified shared representation that is drawn on by ordinary people in everyday circumstances.

Thus Moscovici developed his own account of social representations, which included the following features: 'social representations are cognitive systems with a logic and language of their own . . . They do not represent simply "opinions about", "images of" or "attitudes towards" but "theories" or "branches of knowledge" in their own right, for the discovery and organisation of reality' (Moscovici 1973, p. xii). In addition,

> social representations concern the contents of everyday thinking and the stock of ideas that gives coherence to our religious beliefs, political ideas and the connec- tions we create as spontaneously as we breathe. They make it possible for us to classify persons and objects, to compare and explain behaviours and to objectify them as parts of our social setting. While representations are often to be located in the minds of men and women, they can just as often be found 'in the world', and as such examined separately.
>
> (Moscovici 1988, p. 214)

Furthermore, Moscovici has claimed that social representations can also be described as

> systems of values, ideas and practices with a twofold function: first to establish an order which will enable individuals to orient themselves in their material and social world and to master it; and secondly to take place among the members of a community by providing them with a code for social exchange and a code for naming and classifying unambiguously the various aspects of their worlds and their individual and group history.
>
> (Moscovici 1973, p. xii)

Moscovici (1984, 1988) believed that human beings create a 'thinking society' within which social life is constructed and reconstructed. Representations have a changing, dynamic nature – 'social life in the making'. They are created, sustained and reconstructed by individuals and groups in everyday interaction.

> they lead a life of their own, circulate, merge, attract and repel each other, and give birth to new representations, while old ones die out . . . being shared by all and strengthened by tradition, it constitutes a social reality *sui generis*. The more its origin is forgotten, and its conventional nature ignored, the more fossilized it becomes. That which is ideal gradually becomes materialized.
>
> (Moscovici 1984, p. 13)

According to Moscovici, thinking is done in terms of two processes, anchoring and objectification. *Anchoring* occurs where a new or unfamiliar object is rendered familiar by means of comparing it with a prototype or model that is familiar and culturally accessible. If we decide the new stimuli are similar to the representation we already have, then we will attribute other characteristics of the prototype to them. The object can be readjusted so as to fit in with the prototype. 'The ascendancy of the test case is due . . . to its concreteness, to a kind of vividness which leaves such a deep imprint in our memory that we are able to use it thereafter as a "model" against which we measure individual cases and any image that even remotely resembles it' (Moscovici 1984, p. 32). In other words, giving things names assigns them a place in the societal identity matrix. For example in the UK, the 'model' of disability might be the widely used wheelchair symbol, or the 'model' terminal illness might be cancer or AIDS. These are the sorts of images or ideas that are most readily called to mind when the concept is mentioned.

Objectification is the process by which abstract and unfamiliar ideas are transformed into concrete and 'objective' commonsense reality. As Moscovici (1984) stated, 'To objectify is to discover the iconic quality of an imprecise idea or being, to reproduce a concept in an image' (p. 38). Thus, as a result of the popular appropriation of psychoanalysis, people might believe they have egos, complexes and neuroses. This process of objectification may involve:

1 *Personification.* For example, in the case of psychoanalysis, it might be personified perhaps by Freud. This can be seen at work in other health care disciplines, too, where operations, procedures, instruments and parts of the body come to be known by their originators' names. Fallopian tubes may be grasped with Spencer Wells forceps, for example.

2 *Figuration* occurs where an abstract notion is identified with a metaphorical image. For example, when Moscovici and Hewstone (1983) asked about people's ideas of the European Community, responses came in terms of butter mountains and wine lakes.

3 *Ontologization.* This is where abstract entities and hypothetical constructs are treated as if they were material entities. In health care, we can see this at work where suffering participants come to see their illness as having a real existence, or where healers or sufferers come to define their distress in terms of something that sounds concrete and scientific. Diffuse facial and jawbone pains, once defined as trigeminal neuralgia, take on a much more real quality and, arguably, are more easily dealt with. Furthermore, once it is proposed that the sufferer have an operation to coat the offending nerve in teflon, to prevent it being irritated by surrounding blood vessels, the idea takes on yet another kind of ontologization as something susceptible to technological intervention and possibly cure.

Thus, the general drift of this kind of theorizing is that people will very often be thinking in terms of concrete phenomena, rather than more abstract ones, as a result of these processes of personification, figuration and ontologization.

A number of topics relating to health and illness have been investigated through the framework of social representations theory. Let us review a few examples of this variety of research, as it has something to tell us about the way that concept formulations of health and illness, ideas of the body and their conceptual folkways are constructed, formulated and deployed in everyday explanation.

Our first example of a domain of thinking about the body that has been studied with a view to discerning the social representations involved is the idea of left and right hemispheric specialization in the brain (Moscovici and Hewstone 1983). The pioneering work of Roger Sperry (1913–1994) on 'split brain' patients, for which he earned the Nobel Prize, had placed these issues on the scientific and popular agenda. However, what is equally interesting is how these ideas found their way into everyday language. Here, laypeople can talk readily about which of the hemispheres does what, for example the idea of language in the left, with intuition, emotion and subjective functions allegedly being located in the right. This 'cerebral dualism' is sometimes used in popular parlance to explain a number of other 'dilemmatic' cultural themes, for example femininity versus masculinity, reason versus intuition, even the epithets 'left brained' and 'right brained' used to describe reasoning, strategies for problem solving and styles of living. These concept formulations, then, have a life far in excess of their original formulation in neurology and may appear in a variety of popular discourses about such things as stress, lifestyle and gender. In a sense, the liveliness of the concept formulations occurs because they have long since been liberated from Sperry's laboratory and can take their place in the popular lexicon.

A second example concerns mental health and the idea of madness. This is an especially interesting one because mental ill-health has proved to be especially enigmatic and, despite the efforts of biologically oriented researchers, there are relatively few reliable pegs on which to hang the phenomena in question. In her book *Madness and Social Representations,* Jodelet (1991) describes how people thought about mental illness in a small French community, Ainay-Le-Chateau, where care in the community dates back to the early years of the twentieth century and mentally ill people are housed with 'foster families' as 'lodgers'. As she interviewed people about what they thought 'madness' was about, they would often begin with 'mental illness, I don't know about that' (p. 149). Yet they would also be able to say a great deal about the lodgers and their problems. In particular, the interviewees were often concerned with issues of dirt and contamination. However, in talking about their lodgers' dirtiness, informants also expressed a good deal of loyalty towards them:

> dirtiness seemed to siphon off the major part of the negativity of insanity and is a less disturbing manifestation of the illness than others. Ultimately it is reassuring. One then begins to understand the foster parent who declared, 'a bad lodger is a dirty lodger' and then told us of her oldest one, 'He's been with me for twenty-seven years. He's not bad at all. I'm not frightened of him'. Of course, 'He's dirty I could kill him sometimes. Every day he goes in his trousers'. To have to wash a pair of trousers every day for twenty-seven years! But 'He's not wicked. That's what I'm afraid of I would hate to change. I would prefer to put up with it'. Dirtiness which is due to illness is unthreatening. That alone makes it worth

putting up with, whatever unpleasantness that entails, provided that it does not exceed a limit of revulsion which appears to be quite high.

(Jodelet 1991, pp. 143–4)

Dirtiness, then, could be used to justify the lodger having separate meals from the rest of the family – it was not through prejudice or fear but matters of taste and hygiene.

In the same way, their professed lack of knowledge about mental illness is a strategy for managing the potential threat posed by mental illness: 'It was as if by becoming the object of an explicit knowledge or formulation the power of mental illness to generate anxiety would be released' (Jodelet 1991, p. 150).

The concepts in use here appear to facilitate a particular conceptual and practical way of dealing with the phenomenon. The determined reluctance to formally conceptualize the phenomenon in question is itself a kind of strategy to manage the issue. The absence of concept formulations which explicitly address the symptoms of mental disorder may in itself be an interesting research phenomenon. Sometimes the absence of concepts, or the deflection of the issue by other concept formulations that address different aspects, might, paradoxically, yield a more functional way of dealing with the issue.

However, there are several examples of issues relating to mental health being described much more explicitly by the participants in research designed to elicit the everyday concept formulations of the phenomena. For example, to investigate the 'social representations' of madness in India, Wagner et al. (1999) provided their participants with a brief hypothetical description of a young person who had started behaving strangely and asked participants a series of questions about what they thought the problem might be and what they might do if a member of their own family behaved in this way, whether they would consult a traditional healer or a psychiatrist and if so what would be done. The participants tended to explain the events in terms of (1) family norms and adjustment, (2) ideas of heredity and its moral threat to the family, as well as (3) ideas of ghost or spirit possession:

1   Family issues included such explanations as 'any of his demands was not fulfilled, internally suffocated he wants something, some desire was suppressed inside this can also be a cause' (R33, F) (p. 425). Or, speaking of a case he knew of, another respondent said, 'Yes, there was a famous story about him. Some girl had cheated him in love. He was a fertilizer engineer and the girl's love for him was based on sex. After that her father did not agree to the marriage. He left his job and became mad' (R18, M) (p. 426).

2   The idea of family issues was also prominent in the second theme, but in a slightly different way as this related to notions of heredity and contagion: 'I know such families which have a mentally ill person [among them] and the behaviour of the villagers towards them [families] is not good. People say that he is mad. The second thing is that in villages there is a concept, that if there is one who is mentally ill in a family, the other members will also be mentally ill for sure, because there is a big contribution of the family in making a person mentally ill' (R15, M) (p. 427).

3   The third theme, of ghost and spirit possession, was curious in several ways. Few interviewees admitted to believing in this themselves, though many others said that it is a commonplace belief in their neighbourhood. 'I can only say that there is some invisible power, a ghost possessed him, which was treated by sacred words. Sacred words have power' (R22, M).

> '*Interviewer*: Sir, do you think that those people who are possessed by a ghost cannot be treated by a psychiatrist?
> *Respondent*: No they cannot treat this, only the traditional healer can treat them. These things are out of his [the psychiatrist's] reach' (R22, M) (pp. 430–1).

Thus, concept formulations and social representations are often concerned with the kinds of tools for thinking which participants might use themselves, but they are also concerned with what other people might think; perhaps, as in this case, people who are seen as less advanced and somehow more superstitious. The conceptual machinery is all present and in working order but it is as if the participants do not quite fully endorse it. Thus, sometimes people can appear to be aware of a variety of different possible formulations which might explain events. This theme of diversity and flexibility in terms of the way people might deploy concepts is an important one and we shall return to this later. As well as being able to display this flexibility, it may be that people are aware of the persuasive consequences of adopting one concept formulation rather than another, and of thinking in terms of concrete examples from their own experience or from that of people in their neighbourhood.

There are a number of aspects of the health and illness theme that have been investigated to examine the kinds of concepts and representations which people hold. In a classic study. Herzlich (1973) conducted a series of interviews to determine how middle-class people in France thought of health and illness. Again, there were a number of common themes detectable in the results:

1   The urban way of life was thought to be responsible for a number of complaints, for example because it resulted in fatigue and nervous tension. Food in cities was not considered to be trustworthy either.

2   Illness came from the external environment, whereas the individual was the source of health and healing. In this respect, the social representation of health was rather like the vitalistic notions of the eighteenth and early nineteenth century we mentioned earlier.

3   The individual and his or her relationship with illness was structured around a number of binary oppositions such as internal versus external, healthy versus unhealthy, urban versus rural, natural versus unnatural, individual versus society. For example, in the present day, food advertising often represents rural environments, crops and livestock, rather than the factory setting in which many foodstuffs are manufactured.

4   In Herzlich's study, illnesses themselves were not classified along the same lines as within medicine, but were constructed along lines that were concerned with severity, with whether or not it was painful, the duration of the illness and the nature of its onset.

Whereas this sketch of social representations and some of the work that has been done to elicit the representations groups of people are using to interpret the field of health and illness might seem persuasive, as befits a book with a philosophical bent, we should point out some problems with the idea and the research on which it is based.

First, as Potter and Edwards (1999) argue, social representations theory is primarily about perception and cognition and does not have much to say about action. Potter and Edwards argue that action is central to people's lives and involves the 'enormous range of practical, technical and interpersonal tasks that people perform while living their relationships, doing their jobs, and engaging in various cultural domains' (p. 448). Thus, social representations theory leaves out a substantial amount of human activity and practice.

Second, in social representations theory, the notion of representation is crucial, but these representations are rather passive entities. On the other hand, Potter and Edwards argue that representations in everyday discourse are often highly contrived and constructed entities, as people build their representations through language to persuade, assign blame, elicit agreement and so forth. Language, in other words, is about doing social business, in a way that Wittgenstein would have appreciated, rather than simply representing things. This is partly why we have chosen the term concept formulation, because we wish to alert the reader to the way that conceptualizing things is an active, strategic process and may involve selecting and promoting courses of action too.

Third, social representations theory foregrounds communication, but it does not address the actual communicative process in very much detail. Moscovici disparages conversation as 'babble'. In practice, it is very difficult to examine, say, the transcript of a conversation and see where the messages relating to a particular representation are and how they are being transferred. The representations have a kind of ghostly presence behind the transcript of an interview or a naturally occurring conversation and this prompts sceptics such as Potter and Edwards to ask whether they are instead impositions on the part of the researcher.

Fourth, the emphasis on cognition in social representations theory has made it attractive to social psychologists, because it assumes that people are information processors, storers and retrievers, just like cognitive psychology and philosophy of mind from the 1960s to the present. However, Potter and Edwards say that maybe there is more to cognition than this image of people as information processors allows. Perhaps cognition might instead be going on in conversational interaction as people formulate thoughts, memories, feelings and intuitions – and maybe even concepts – jointly through interpersonal processes. It may not be the case that cognitions neatly live inside someone's head in any simple sense.

So, to assess what this all means for making sense of health care research, health care practice and how to think about these issues, we shall pause to assess what can be learned from this approach. For example, we might deduce that arguments work best if they are ontologized and exemplified with things that the people concerned find easy to visualize or think of as entities. It also tells us, if we step back slightly, that this is a way of making sense of thinking processes themselves. Whereas it has largely been used with everyday concepts, it could also be used with more esoteric concepts in

health care and could even go some way towards addressing the problem of studying expertise that we identified above.

Lay theories and everyday explanations

A related strand of work which aims to elicit the kinds of concepts that people hold concerning health and illness is that of 'lay theories'. As the name suggests, this involves a systematic investigation of the sorts of folk theories which are likely to be held by the layperson. This area of work has been contributed largely by Adrian Furnham and colleagues (e.g. Furnham 1988; Furnham and Cheng 2000; Furnham and Murao 2000; Furnham et al. 2001), but a number of other researchers have entered the fray to discover the cognitive structure of everyday concepts, beliefs, theories and explanations.

To give a flavour of this kind of research as it impacts on concepts relevant to health, let us consider a paper by Mercado-Martinez and Ramos-Herrera (2002) concerning lay beliefs about diabetes in Mexico. Among their sample of Mexican diabetics, it was clear that their theories about how their condition had started did not correspond with current medical thinking. Participants tended to attribute their condition to social and emotional circumstances linked to life events and experiences, with men tending to focus on work and social circumstances outside the home, while women tended to mention family life and their domestic settings. This was rather different to the kinds of explanations for diabetes reported in the English-speaking world, where people's explanations tend to incorporate more contemporary bio-medical thinking. According to Garro (1995) and Kay (1979), Anglophone sufferers were likely to attribute diabetes to food, diet heredity and stress. Moreover, in South America, people have been noted to believe that diabetes is a result of an episode of fright (susto) (Rubel et al. 1992). Although Mercado-Martinez and Ramos-Herrera's (2002) participants did not specifically mention the idea of fright, they were in many cases concerned that drinking while in an intense emotional state – anger, surprise, fear or suffering – had brought on diabetes.

From investigations such as this, it is claimed by some critics of the health care system that it would be beneficial if health care providers were to move away from an authoritative role as providers of information and knowledge and instead search for a model that incorporates the voices, concepts and concerns of the diverse social actors who are involved in the process of health care (Hunt et al. 1998). That is, it is felt from this perspective that perhaps things would be better if all parties participated in the construction of alternatives. In the case of diabetes in Mexico, in particular, the authors believed that including the perspectives of poor individuals who attribute their illnesses to their material, economic and emotional circumstances might have a dramatic effect on the provision of health care in Mexico and, indeed, the rest of the world.

Concept formulations, then, can be seen as powerful agents of change. They may reflect the voices, world-views and economic interests of sections of society, some of whom may have hitherto been systematically marginalized in health care research and practice. Thus, the study of lay theories of health and illness, which often begins as a psychological enquiry, may lead to sociological issues and from there to political and ethical concerns.

The question of where the various lay theories or concepts of a health issue will lead is even more acute when we look at the situation within the UK. As the diversity of cultures, experiences and world-views intermingle, this presents enormous challenges in providing a health care system that is geared to the diversity of the population. In addition, when we consider how this culturally diverse population is also shot through with inequality, racism and misogyny, the problems appear even more intractable. If we take the issue of mental health, it is worth noting that this is one area where there has been acute controversy. Let us illustrate the issue by looking at the disproportionate number of young black men who are diagnosed as suffering from schizophrenia (Harrison *et al.* 1984; Jones and Gray 1986; Lewis *et al.* 1990). There are concerns that this over-representation of young black men in this category may result from the attitudes and values of psychiatrists (Lewis *et al.* 1990), or that the kinds of experiences and practices of this group, particularly of a religious nature, place them at risk of being diagnosed with schizophrenia when judged against a white, middle-class, Euro-American nosological system (Kiev 1964; Pote and Orrell 2002). Indeed, in Kiev's classic study in the early 1960s, of 100 Afro-Caribbean youths questioned, almost all had some experience of religious or magical experiences that could be called 'delusional' when judged against psychiatric criteria. In the light of these concerns, Pote and Orrell (2002) examined the ideas of different ethnic groups in the UK about mental health and illness in a study of lay representations in an ethnically and culturally diverse sample. Compared with the white population, participants of Bangladeshi origin were less likely to identify suspiciousness or hallucinations as signs of mental illness and people of Afro-Caribbean origin were the least likely to view unusual thought content as indicative of mental illness. This difference between people of Afro-Caribbean origin and the majority white population, the authors argued, is important in making sense of the former's higher rate of diagnosis. Moreover, if a client's and psychiatrist's fundamental concepts of mental disorder differ, it will be that much more difficult for productive therapeutic alliances to be formed. Indeed, by looking at case notes, Johnson and Orrell (1996) detected that psychiatrists were much more likely to say that their white patients had 'insight' whereas their black ones did not. This was independent of the severity of symptoms and reflects, the authors surmised, the differing world-views of mental illness held by psychiatry on the one hand and the Afro-Caribbean population on the other. Thus, looking at the concepts held by different groups in the arena of health care could have some important implications for how we address clients themselves and how we address the larger-scale structure of health inequalities within which they are embedded.

The reader might wish to contrast this example with the case of cranial osteopathy we mentioned earlier. There, the fact that the practitioner and the clients seemed to be at loggerheads in terms of how they conceptualized what was going on didn't seem to matter. Indeed, it might have even made the social business of therapy easier. In the case of psychiatry and ethnicity though, it appears that the lack of commonality between the service providers and some client groups may contribute to the latter's disadvantage in the mental health care system. Certainly, there is a good deal of literature to suggest that consensus and coherence is an important issue. For example, Kitson (1993) argued that the best concepts are those which result when 'all

the different concepts of a thing coincide'. Certainly, this might make communication easier but is consensus always a good thing? What if the young black men diagnosed with schizophrenia and those who cared for them shared the same concept formulations as the largely white psychiatric establishment? What if they believed that they were indeed mad and required treatment? A lack of consensus perhaps offers the possibility that concepts might be formulated differently and less oppressively.

What does it mean for us? Philosophy and research in practice

After having considered all these different ideas that have impacted on the conceptualization of nature, the formulation of research questions, research design and making sense of the results, it is appropriate to examine what it means for our lives as researchers, practitioners and theorists.

One of the important features of present-day life is that it is often possible to detect intriguing contradictions between different belief systems, moralities, styles of life and compartments of experience. To make sense of this and explain what it means in more detail, let us take some examples from our own lifeworlds as scholars and citizens to help identify some of these disjunctures and contradictions. Thus, let us consider what we three authors think we are doing as we conduct research, attempt to get it published, and sustain positions in UK universities.

One of us, Brian Brown, is in his spare time an amateur engineer and metallurgist as well as a would-be performance artist, yet in his academic life he describes himself as a 'nosebleed antifoundationalist' and subscribes to analytic positions that challenge the very physical substrate on which he works. His experiments with physical materials and objects are motivated by a kind of curiosity as to the kinds of forces they will sustain, yet the emotional and perceptual effects on the audience are important too. In his exhibition work as an artist, he tries to create visual effects with architectural materials that mix up the audience and juxtapose things that are usually seen in different parts of buildings and include images of rejuvenation with images of decay. Doing research and getting things published is about playing a kind of game whose rules are largely opaque but which are implemented by people like journal editors and referees as well as people on RAE panels, all of whom have to be satisfied, but at the same time it is important to install something of oneself in published work too. Especially if it is an idea which is subversive or which has not appeared in print before. There is a great deal of satisfaction to be had in smuggling things past the gatekeepers.

Carolyn Hicks, who has perhaps been the most successful academically, being the only one of the three of us to have achieved a professorship, has this to say about the relationship between her work as a researcher and her awareness of philosophy:

> I could not honestly say that the philosophical principles underpinning the scientific method consciously impinge on my research activities. Despite my theoretical commitment to Popper's theory of falsification, my aim usually is to find support for the hypothesis; I certainly rarely think of submitting an article for publication unless I have significant results. In view of this mismatch, there is a clear dissonance between my values, what I do and what I say. I have been

pressured by the RAE to publish, publish, publish and seduced by the implicit journal rules that state that publication is more likely if the results are significant. Therefore, because I am bound by the political, organizational and occupational contexts that place these demands on academics, I do exactly the opposite of what Popper would claim is the real route to truth. I am therefore subverting the proper scientific process and my own principles to boot. There is also, of course, the human need for affirmation. To proceed down the route towards falsification is a negative human experience, even if it is ultimately positive for scientific truth. Despite my constant reassurances to my postgraduate students that getting non-significant results is just as valuable as getting significant ones, their anxiety about obtaining support for the hypothesis is a constant reminder that despite all Popper's logic, it doesn't hold much sway for the researcher, and especially the novice researcher. Indeed, my experience suggests that obtaining non-significant results can act as a serious deterrent to conducting any more research. In an era of evidence-based health care, where the corpus of sound research needed to inform all levels and types of practice is woefully inadequate, this would seem to be counterproductive. It is philosophical dilemma, with philosophy and health/academic research seemingly serving two different masters.

Another of us, Paul Crawford, has a variety of different backgrounds. A one-time trainee Roman Catholic priest, he has also been a nurse and is a novelist who is currently working in fields as diverse as nursing, English literature and journalism. One of his pieces of fiction may soon become a film or television drama. Again, this diversity of interests brings with it new insights as well as frustrations. He is constrained by the needs of the nursing degree curriculum in a university context but at the same time is attracted to teaching literature, developing new courses exploiting new media. Overall, the need to attract external funding if one is to succeed these days in a UK university is a powerful one and seems to be the key to career advancement and promotion.

These brief biographical fragments of what we do and how we sustain our lives in the UK university context are also tempered by the increase in student numbers, the sight of so many of our colleagues becoming ill with stress-related cardiovascular disorders and the difficulty in coping with increasing numbers of directives from within both the university system and the health care system. The difficulty in putting down roots and making links with other bodies such as health care providers and service users is complicated even further by the high turnover of personnel and the frequent reorganizations. One of Brown's PhD students has seen the health care organizations she is studying transform out of all recognition in the space of three years. This, then, places additional constraints on the kinds of research we can do. Yet at the same time it opens up opportunities for research designs and forms of understanding that have yet to be invented.

Despite all this disruption and fragmentation, it appears to us that the ideology of the health care services remains relentlessly modernist and continues to be dominated by medically trained practitioners and researchers whose perspective on life is usually modernist too. It is easy to gain the impression that as far as they are concerned, theirs is the only truth; that they are the ones with the privileged expert knowledge base; and

that their preferred methodology is the scientific one. In other words, health care and health care research still have a prevailing ethos that there is only one view and only one true, objective perspective. On the other hand, nursing, along with the other non-medical professions, embraces the notion of multiple perspectives more readily and, in this way, is certainly more postmodernist than the medical professions. This predilection for multiple perspectives and methodologies also challenges more readily the grand narrative of the medical profession. Two of us (B.B. and C.H.) were originally taught in the modernist scientific spirit and have more or less wandered off the path. From an early attachment to the scientific method, C.H. has moved to a multiple methodology and multiple-perspective viewpoint, going for method triangulation where possible, because she believes it provides the richest picture and the most accurate information. B.B. disputes that anything can be 'accurate' in any simple sense because the notion of accuracy itself is subject to judgement and relies on very many assumptions and taken-for-granteds concerning how the world should be conceptualized, seen and measured. Thus, he would see the knowledge creation process itself as a topic of enquiry. In this view, the interesting things about nature are created by humans doing things together, rather than simply heating things and hammering them.

All three of us would probably agree that experience cannot easily be quantified or broken down into fragments about which one can generate meaningful hypotheses or collect numerical data, because it is too varied, complicated and subjective. Yet it is this very experience that seems to provide the insights and explanations needed to interpret the quantitative data that we generate. The process of making the numbers mean something is much more difficult to explain. So, in some ways our own research approaches fit neatly with the postmodernist agenda, though we have not necessarily moved in that direction because postmodernism was persuasive, but rather because of the circumstances within which we work and an affinity with the belief that in complex systems there can be multiple solutions and answers and, therefore, our understanding may be enriched if we use multiple approaches.

It is also apposite to consider whether there are any implications here for teaching the value of a philosophical approach to research in the academy, the clinic, the community or on a training course. In a sense, people are adroit at adjudicating between competing truth claims. An exercise one of us (B.B.) sometimes uses with students is to say to them, 'A funny thing happened to me yesterday. I saw a flying saucer and the aliens came out and abducted me and took me back into the spaceship and did experiments on me and stuck probes in my you-know-what. Now if someone said that to you, would you believe it?' Most people say no. Then we attempt to generate some discussion as to why this is a difficult thing to believe, what would make it convincing (part of the spaceship perhaps?) and what other explanations there are for this kind of experience. The aim is to mobilize and examine the kinds of folk epistemologies that students bring to the educational encounter. In this way, we are perhaps coming close to the educational process that Northrop Frye envisaged:

> The teacher, as has been recognized at least since Plato's Meno, is not primarily someone who knows instructing someone who does not know. He [sic] is rather someone who attempts to re-create the subject in the student's mind, and

his strategy in doing this is first of all to get the student to recognize what he already potentially knows, which includes breaking up the powers of repression in his mind that keep him from knowing what he knows.

(Frye 1982, p. xv)

Part of generating this kind of philosophical awareness on the part of students and beginning researchers, then, is to get them to recognize what they are already doing in evaluating knowledge, making inferences and creating credible stories of their own.

One of the fundamental techniques that underlies traditional variants of positivism and falsificationism and has also played a key role in realist and postmodernist philosophies, is reformulating what we know as a set of questions or problems that we can then go on to solve. Whether we treat these as research questions from which we can deduce testable hypotheses or use them as more speculative thought experiments – as 'what if' and 'as if' statements – will play a key role in our enquiry. Getting people to think of the world around them in terms of questions is perhaps the breakthrough that turns them into thinkers. This centrality of questions to the educational and research processes has been recognized by other thinkers on educational topics too. Here is Neil Postman, writing in his book *Teaching as a Conserving Activity*:

all our knowledge results from questions, which is another way of saying that question-asking is our most important intellectual tool. I would go so far as to say that the answers we carry about in our heads are largely meaningless unless we know the questions which produced them . . . What, for example, are the sorts of questions that obstruct the mind, or free it, in the study of history? How are these questions different from those one might ask of a mathematical proof, or a literary work, or a biological theory? What students need to know are the rules of discourse which comprise the subject, and among the most central of such rules are those which govern what is and what is not a legitimate question.

(Postman 1979, p. 23)

In other words, it is not so much the solutions we come up with but the kinds of questions we ask that creates us as thinkers. Thus, the ability to turn experience into questions is the hallmark of the kind of mindset we are trying to convey. Perhaps among these final words it would be apposite to quote the late C. Wright Mills, who had a firm grasp on the possibilities inherent in human enquiry. What he had to say about sociological research has a good deal in common with what we are encouraging:

Neither the life of an individual nor the history of a society can be understood without understanding both. Yet men [*sic*] do not usually define the troubles they endure in terms of historical change and institutional contradiction . . . The sociological imagination enables its possessor to understand the larger historical scene in terms of its meaning for the inner life and the external career of a variety of individuals . . . The first fruit of this imagination – and the first lesson of the social science that embodies it – is the idea that the individual can understand his own experience and gauge his own fate only by locating himself within this period, that he can know his own chances in life only by becoming aware of those of all

individuals in his circumstances . . . We have come to know that every individual lives, from one generation to the next, in some society; that he lives out a biography, and that he lives it out within some historical sequence.

(Mills 1959, pp. 3–10)

The details of individual experience and individual biographies, from heart transplants to ingrowing toenails, and from mild disaffection to florid psychosis, are intelligible in this view if we examine the context and look at the experience as part of an individual's biography. They also become understandable if we step back and look at them in the general context of the society and the culture where the troubles are taking place. In this way, perhaps the experience of ill health can be made meaningful by the researcher and hence to the sufferer too. The concluding words concerning what we are trying to advocate within health care research should perhaps go to Arthur Kleinman (1988; Schweizer 1995), taken from his book *The Illness Narratives*:

> clinical and behavioural science research . . . possess no category to describe suffering, no routine way of recording this most thickly human dimension of patients' and families' stories of experiencing illness. Symptom scales and survey questionnaires and behavioural checklists quantify functional impairment and disability, rendering the quality of life fungible.
>
> (Kleinman 1988, p. 17)

Medical – or even nursing – categories however are woefully insufficient to account for the experience of illness:

> [A]bout suffering they are silent. The thinned out image of patients and families which perforce must emerge from such research is scientifically replicable but ontologically invalid; it has statistical, not epistemological significance; it is a dangerous distortion.
>
> (Kleinman 1988, p. 17)

Kleinman himself, as a practitioner, sees his job as to *delay* the naming of the illness so as to 'legitimiz[e] the patient's illness experience – authorizing that experience, auditing it empathetically' (p. 17). Indeed, 'we should be willing to stop at that point where validity becomes uncertain' (p. 74).

Or, as one of the major twentieth-century thinkers who tried to understand inhumanity and suffering, Theodor Adorno puts it, capturing a final paradox:

> Reason can subsume suffering under concepts, it can furnish means to alleviate suffering; but it can never express suffering in the medium of experience, for to do so would be irrational by reason's own standards. Therefore, even when it is understood, suffering remains mute and inconsequential.
>
> (Adorno 1984, p. 27)

There is a great deal yet to be understood.

References

Abbott, S., Johnson, L. and Lewis, H. (2001) Participation in arranging continuing health care packages: experiences and aspirations of service users, *Journal of Nursing Management*, 9: 79–85.

Adorno, T.W. (1984) *Aesthetic Theory* (translated by C. Lenhardt). London: Routledge.

Aspis, S. (1997) Self-advocacy for people with learning difficulties: does it have a future?, *Disability and Society*, 12(4): 501–11.

Benner, P. (1982) Issues in competency-based testing, *Nursing Outlook*, May, pp. 303–9.

Benner, P. (1984) *From Novice to Expert: Excellence and Power in Clinical Nursing*. Menlo Park, CA: Addison-Wesley.

Benner, P. (1992) *From Beginner to Expert: Clinical Knowledge in Critical Care Nursing*. Athens, OH: Fuld Institute for Technology in Nursing Education (video).

Benner, P. and Tanner, C. (1987) Clinical judgement: how expert nurses use intuition, *American Journal of Nursing*, 87(1): 23–31.

Benner, P. and Wrubel, J. (1989) *The Primacy of Caring Stress and Coping in Health and Illness*. Menlo Park, CA: Addison-Wesley.

Bonner, G., Lowe, T., Rawcliffe, D. and Wellman, N. (2002) Trauma for all: a pilot study of the subjective experience of physical restraint for mental health inpatients and staff in the UK, *Journal of Psychiatric and Mental Health Nursing*, 8: 465–73.

Carper, B. (1978) Fundamental patterns of knowing in nursing, *Advances in Nursing Science*, 1(1): 13–23.

Darling, H. (1995) Satisfying a hunger: a personal journey of self discovery through further nursing education, *Nursing Praxis*, 10(1): 12–21.

Davies, D. (2000) Sex and the relationship facilitation project for people with disabilities, *Sexuality and Disability*, 18(3): 187–94.

Dreyfus, H.L. (1979) *What Computers Can't Do*. New York: Harper & Row.

Dreyfus, H.L. and Dreyfus, S.E. (1985) *Mind Over Machine: The Power of Human Intuition and Expertise in the Era of the Computer*. New York: Free Press/Macmillan.

Frye, N. (1982) *The Great Code: The Bible and Literature*. New York: Harcourt Brace & Co.

Furnham, A. (1988) *Lay Theories: Everyday Understanding of Problems in the Social Sciences*. Oxford: Pergamon Press.

Furnham, A. and Cheng, H. (2000) Lay theories of happiness, *Journal of Happiness Studies*, 1(2): 227–46.

Furnham, A. and Murao, M. (2000) A cross cultural comparison of British and Japanese lay theories of schizophrenia, *International Journal of Social Psychiatry*, 46(1): 4–20.

Furnham, A., Pereira, E. and Rawles, R. (2001) Lay theories of psychotherapy: perceptions of the efficacy of different cures for specific disorders, *Psychology, Health and Medicine*, 6(1): 77–84.

Gardner, H. (1983) *Frames of Mind: The Theory of Multiple Intelligences*. London: Heinemann.

Garro, L. (1995) Individual or societal responsibility? Explanations of diabetes in an Anishinaabe (Ojibway) community, *Social Science and Medicine*, 40(1): 37–46.

Gerth, H. and Mills, C.W. (1964) *Character and Social Structure*. New York: Harbinger.

Goffman, E. (1961) *Asylums*. New York: Anchor.

Harrison, G., Ineichen, B., Smith, J. and Morgan, H.G. (1984) Psychiatric hospital admissions in Bristol. II. Social and clinical aspects of compulsory admission, *British Journal of Psychiatry*, 145: 605–11.

Herzlich, C. (1973) *Health and Illness: A Social Psychological Analysis*. London: Academic Press.

Holden, D. and Smart, D. (1999) Adding value to the patient experience in emergency medi-

cine: what features of the emergency department visit are most important to patients?, *Emergency Medicine*, 1: 3–8.

Hunt, L., Valenzuela, M. and Pugh, J. (1998) *Porque me toco a mi?* Mexican American diabetes patients' causal stories and their relationship to treatment behaviours, *Social Science and Medicine*, 46: 959–69.

Jodelet, D. (1991) *Madness and Social Representations*. Hemel Hempstead: Harvester Wheatsheaf.

Johns, C. (1995a) The value of reflective practice for nursing, *Journal of Clinical Nursing*, 4(1): 23–30.

Johns, C. (1995b) Framing learning through reflection with Carper's fundamental ways of knowing in nursing, *Journal of Advanced Nursing*, 22(2): 226–34.

Johnson, S. and Orrell, M. (1996) Insight, psychosis and ethnicity: a case note study, *Psychological Medicine*, 26: 1081–4.

Jones, B.E. and Gray, B.A. (1986) Problems in diagnosing schizophrenia and affective disorders amongst blacks, *Hospital and Community Psychiatry*, 37: 61–5.

Kay, M. (1979) Health and illness in a Mexican American barrio, in E. Spicer (ed.) *Ethnic Medicine in the Southwest*. Tuscon, AZ: University of Arizona Press.

Kiev, A. (1964) *Magic, Faith and Healing*. New York: Free Press.

Kitson, A. (ed.) (1993) *Nursing Art and Science*. London: Chapman & Hall.

Kleinman, A. (1988) *The Illness Narratives: Suffering, Healing and the Human Condition*. New York: Basic Books.

Lathlean, J. and Vaughan, B. (1994) *Unifying Nursing Practice and Theory*. Oxford: Butterworth Heinemann.

Lewis, G., Croft Jeffreys, C. and David, A. (1990) Are British psychiatrists racist?, *British Journal of Psychiatry*, 157: 410–15.

Lumby, J. (1991) Threads of an emerging discipline: praxis, reflection, rhetoric and research, in G. Gray and R. Pratt (eds) *Towards a Discipline of Nursing*. Melbourne, VIC: Churchill-Livingstone.

Mercado-Martinez, F.J. and Ramos-Herrera, I.M. (2002) Diabetes: the layperson's theories of causality, *Qualitative Health Research*, 12(6): 792–806.

Mills, C.W. (1959) *The Sociological Imagination*. New York: Oxford University Press.

Moscovici, S. (1973) Foreword, in C. Herzlich, *Health and Illness: A Social Psychological Analysis*. London: Academic Press.

Moscovici, S. (1976) *La Psychoanalyse: Son Image et Son Public* (revised edition). Paris: Presses Universitaires de France.

Moscovici, S. (1984) The phenomenon of social representations, in R.M. Farr and S. Moscovici (eds) *Social Representations*. Cambridge/Paris: Cambridge University Press/ Maison des Sciences de l'Homme.

Moscovici, S. (1988) Notes towards a description of social representations, *European Journal of Social Psychology*, 18: 211–80.

Moscovici, S. and Hewstone, M. (1983) Social representations and social explanation: from the naive to the amateur scientist, in M. Hewstone (ed.) *Attribution Theory: Social and Functional Extensions*. Oxford: Blackwell.

Paterson, B. (1991) *Excellence and Expertise in Nursing*. Melbourne, VIC: Deakin University Press.

Peplau, H. (1952) *Interpersonal Relations in Nursing*. New York: GP Putnam's Sons.

Popper, K.R. ([1935] 1959) *The Logic of Scientific Discovery*. London: Hutchinson.

Postman, N. (1979) *Teaching as a Conserving Activity*. New York: Bantam Dell Doubleday.

Pote, H.L. and Orrell, M.W. (2002) Perceptions of schizophrenia in multi-cultural Britain, *Ethnicity and Health*, 7(1): 7–20.

Potter, J. and Edwards, D. (1999) Social representations and discursive psychology: from cognition to action, *Culture and Psychology*, 5(4): 447–58.

Rew, L. (1988) Intuition in decision making, *Image: The Journal of Nursing Scholarship*, 20(3): 150–4.

Rosen, R.D. (1977) *Psychobabble: Fast Talk and Quick Cure in the Era of Feeling*. New York: Athaneum Press.

Rubel, A., O'Nell, C. and Collado, R. (1992) *Introduccion al susto*, in R. Campos (ed.) *La anthropologia medicia en Mexico*. Mexico: Instituto Mora/Universidad Autonoma Metropolitana.

Schraeder, B. and Fischer, D. (1986) Using intuitive knowledge to make clinical decisions, *Maternal Child Nursing*, 2: 161–2.

Schweizer, H. (1995) To give suffering a language, *Literature and Medicine*, 14(2): 210–21.

Wagner, W., Duveen, G., Themel, M. and Verma, J. (1999) The modernisation of tradition: thinking about madness in Patna, India, *Culture and Psychology*, 5(4): 413–45.

Warelow, P. (1997) A nursing journey through discursive praxis, *Journal of Advanced Nursing*, 26(6): 1020–7.

White, J. (1995) Patterns of knowing: review, critique, and update, *Advances in Nursing Science*, 17(4): 73–86.

Wilkes, L. (1991) Phenomenology: a window to the nursing world, in G. Gray and R. Pratt (eds) *Towards a Discipline of Nursing*. Melbourne, VIC: Churchill Livingstone.

Index

THINKING NURSING

Tom Mason and Elizabeth Whitehead

- Important new nursing theory textbook

This major new text seeks to provide nursing students with an accessible overview of the theory which informs the application of nursing activity. The key disciplines that contribute to the nursing curriculum – such as sociology, psychology, public health, economic science and politics – are comprehensively discussed, with each chapter offering both a theoretical discussion and a section showing how the topic in question applies to nursing practice. Particular attention has been paid to pedagogy with brief boxed case studies, chapter summaries, glossaries of key words and further reading lists enabling easy use by students.

Contents:
Introduction – Thinking Sociology – Thinking Psychology – Thinking Anthropology – Thinking Public Health – Thinking Philosophy – Thinking Economics – Thinking Politics – Thinking Science – Thinking Writing – Conclusions – References – Index.

432pp   0 335 21040 6 (Paperback)   0 335 21041 4 (Hardback)

RESEARCH METHODS IN HEALTH
INVESTIGATING HEALTH AND HEALTH SERVICES

Ann Bowling

Praise for the first edition of *Research Methods in Health*:

> . . . a brilliantly clear documentation of different philosophies, approaches and methods of research about health and services. Laid out in an accessible and manageable way, it covers an enormous amount of material without sacrificing thoroughness . . . I would recommend it to a broad readership.
>
> *MIDIRS Midwifery Digest*

> . . . This major research textbook is as good as an introduction to the field as you are likely to find.
>
> *The International Journal of Social Psychiatry*

> . . . an easy to read book with excellent background information on the theory and practice of research. A summary of main points, key terms and recommended reading follows each chapter and there is a useful glossary of terms at the end of the book for quick reference . . . I particularly liked the checklists when undertaking literature reviews and writing research proposals.
>
> *British Journal of Health Care Management*

This new edition of Ann Bowling's well-known and highly respected text has been thoroughly revised and updated to reflect key methodological developments in health research. It is a comprehensive, easy to read guide to the range of methods used to study and evaluate health and health services. It describes the concepts and methods used by the main disciplines involved in health research, including: demography, epidemiology, health economics, psychology and sociology.

The research methods described cover the assessment of health needs, morbidity and mortality trends and rates, costing health services, sampling for survey research, cross-sectional and longitudinal survey design, experimental methods and techniques of group assignment, questionnaire design, interviewing techniques, coding and analysis of quantitative data, methods and analysis of qualitative observational studies, and types of unstructured interviewing.

With new material on topics such as cluster randomization, utility analyses, patients' preferences, and perception of risk, the text is aimed at students and researchers of health and health services. It has also been designed for health professionals and policy makers who have responsibility for applying research findings in practice, and who need to know how to judge the value of that research.

Contents
Part one: Investigating health services and health: the scope of research – Part two: The philosophy, theory and practice of research – Part three: Quantitative research: sampling and research methods – Part four: The tools of quantitative research – Part five: Qualitative and combined research methods, and their analysis – Index.

512pp   0 335 20643 3 (Paperback)   0 335 20644 1 (Hardback)

KEY CONCEPTS AND DEBATES IN HEALTH AND SOCIAL POLICY

Nigel Malin, Stephen Wilmot and Jill Manthorpe

This book identifies key social policy concepts and explores their relevance for health and welfare policy, and for the practice of professionals such as nurses and social workers who are involved in the delivery of services and provision. The text adopts ideologies of welfare approach using examples of recent policy shifts to illustrate theoretical and political tensions. This shift in emphasis away from the traditional approach of documenting policy areas is an important feature of the book. The concepts are organized in terms of doctrinal contests. This allows the authors to explore the tension between different approaches and ways of defining social policy. The aim is to help professionals identify these tensions, to be aware of the strategic choices which have been made in national and agency policy, and to locate their own practice in relationship to these choices. It draws upon the continuing debate around the Third Way and New Labour policies as they apply to health and social welfare; and identifies tensions within a non-ideological, pragmatic set of practices.

Key Concepts and Debates in Health and Social Policy has been written with students and practitioners in mind. It is a valuable resource for a wide range of health and welfare professionals, especially in nursing, social work and occupational therapy. It is also suitable for use on professional training courses, and with students of social policy and health studies.

Contents

Introduction – The Third Way: a distinct approach? – Identifying the Health Problem: need or risk? – Responsibility and Solidarity – Consumerism or Empowerment? – Central Planning and Market Competition – Controlling Service Delivery: professionalism versus managerialism – Community Care and Family Policy – Evaluating Services: quality assurance and the quality debate – Prioritizing and Rationing – Conclusion – Index.

176pp   0 335 19905 4 (Paperback)   0 335 19906 2 (Hardback)